# BUSINESS NETWORKS:

## Concepts, methodologies & research

**1st Edition**

**Global**South
PRESS

Book design by **Héctor Guzmán**

**Giglio, Ernesto**

# BUSINESS NETWORKS:
Concepts, methodologies & research

Includes Bibliographical references and Index

ISBN:
978-1-943350-15-5

1. Networks- 2. Business - 3.Management Science-4. Business Administration.

**Raising**South

P R E S S

## Editorial Board:

Dear Readers:

We are pleased to present the ideas and research under development by the Business Networks group of the Master in Business Management at Universidade Paulista - UNIP. The group consists of five PhD professors who develop research projects in new concepts for new ways of managing business networks. It is a vanguard program in Brazil, fully dedicated to study the phenomenon of networks, comprising a set of disciplines to prepare Msc students in their dissertations.

This book presents a general outcome of recent research conducted by the group. Topics such as power, governance, trust, commitment, innovation, knowledge, clusters, supply chains, network strategies and research methods are discussed. Each topic is developed in a different chapter, and has its backbone in research conducted by the professors and their students. Thus the reader finds both the theory, as well as research practices of networks. Examples involve a number of sectors, such as aviation, housing cooperative, ceramics businesses, famous motorcycle brands, family farming and restaurant chains networks.

With the active collaboration of GlobalSouth Press, we begin a publishing partnership to open space for discussion on networks and its manifestations. Society itself is rapidly evolving into more complex networks, whether on business, cooperation, public and social policies; which require specialized complex studies. We hope to contribute to this in the next few pages.

We wish you an enjoyable and enlightening reading.

Ernesto M. Giglio
Book editor

# Chapter 1.
## Networks: The facts, the format, the concepts.

**Ernesto M. Giglio,**
**Flávio R. Macau**

The discussion about the phenomenon of networks has swelled, mainly on the concepts on the main statement that defines it, the clarity about the subject matter and the ways of researching the various networks manifestations (Dwyer, Schurr, Oh, 1987; Nohria, Eccles, 1992; Gulati, 1995; Hakansson, Snehota, 1995; Ebers, Jarillo, 1998; Castells, 1999; Cinner, Bodin, 2010; Glasbergen, 2010).

Networks theories were initially built with some economic studies, as the Italian agglomerations and the Toyota system, but soon they became popular in the 1980s, with the movement of mergers and acquisitions. Gradually, the area has incorporated the concepts of social networking, which is an old term in Sociology and it was generalizing its vision that all organizations operate in networks (Nohria, Eccles, 1992). In the last two decades the vision extended to arrangements for coordination of government programs, especially in health, tourism and family agriculture.

A convergent statement from the authors who follow this trail is that it is not sufficient to use rational and economic models for understanding the networks, as predominantly occurs in work on supply chain networks, or phenomena of mergers and franchises. It is necessary to use the complexity assumptions that can embrace the unpredictability of the dynamics of the networks phenomenon and models that seek to integrate the variability of human relationships, and the range between the social, economic, political and institutional.

Literature about networks and their manifestations refer to this format being different from hierarchy and market formats. The market format implies that participants follow the guidelines of the isolated competition model; that is, every organization seeks to resolve its resource dependency and create their competitive capabilities.

Therefore, they will always search for the best condition by modifying their suppliers and their markets as their strategies. Working together only occurs while it is beneficial for the organization. Highly competitive markets such as electronics or real estate would be examples. It's everyone for itself and only the best survive.

The hierarchy format suggests that participants follow the guidelines of the model of power clearly established, and the standards and rules created by some to be followed by others. A head office and subsidiaries of an organization would be an example. Even though each subsidiary has a degree of freedom, it must follow the rules laid by the central command. Programs of public policies, in case there is need of cooperative action between the government and society; would be another example. Despite the possibility of the local government to create deployment modes, the guidelines and results should be followed without changes. Here cooperation and joint work is not a collective and harmonious decision, it is a must.

The network format implies that participants follow the guidelines of the efforts of collective action, to address both their collective problems as individual goals. A cooperative of small producers of strawberry would be an example, as each one cannot solve all complex business problems by themselves, and together the power of action can achieve a solution point.

At this point there is an operational concern: In what way can someone know whether a given organizational field, with a number of organizations, is or not organized in network format?

Considering some years of work of the research group in networks of the Master's program in Business Administration from the Universidade Paulista-UNIP, our contribution to this concern is that there are some categories whose presence is strongly related to the network format. This statement is based on numerous literature reviews we and our students have conducted, the sources where these categories ever appears. We have also carried out research where these categories spontaneously arise as foundations (pillars) of the network format. When not present, the signs of market formats (isolated competition), or hierarchy (central power determining the processes) are clearly seen.

These categories are: Interdependence; Complexity; Exchange's Needs; Awareness of the need for collective action; Existence of Collective Objectives; Presence of some rules or norms of joint action (technically called governance). Let's look at them in detail.

## 1.1 Interdependence.

Interdependence is the result of the organizations specialization. In previous decades, it was even possible for a company to cover a wide range of products and services, for the purpose of serving numerous markets. With the evolution of technology allowing production on demand, and consumer awareness on the possibilities for customized products with increasing competition in all sectors; organizations have been specializing in certain products and services, requiring more and more help from other organizations. This help can be in the production line, or in all kinds of support (legal, communications, controls, relations with the union and government, Internet action, to name a few).

Interdependence is also manifested in supply chains such as automotive, where many organizations are in charge of various steps to depend on each other, leading to joint work.

By analyzing a number of organizations, we need to investigate the nature of this interdependence (if it is in the process, support, marketing, or other), and how to solve and prosecute this interdependence (for example, if it takes very detailed cooperation agreements, or if it is a partnership that lasts as long as it serves one party, which it would be more characteristic of market format).

The interdependence is related to complexity.

## 1.2 Complexity.

Complexity determines that the production process of a good or service of a company cannot be accomplished (it is not possible) without the participation of others. The generation of the product or service requires the joint effort of several organizations. The financial system is an easy example to understand: when a person inserts her debit card to make a withdrawal at a terminal, she triggers several interconnected processes, several companies, such as the connection system (IT companies), bank data (bank company), the cash available checking system (logistics companies) and the call center in case of an emergency (telemarketers). A failure in one of them makes the service (the withdrawal) almost impossible.

As businesses are becoming increasingly complicated for legislation, quality control, care in use and handling details; there is need for a joint work that is very much a collective construction (for example a business working plan for sales on the Internet), than a classic system of supplier and purchaser (market format), or a hierarchical system where a central company (as the bank) gives guidelines (the hierarchy format).

When complexity is investigated, it seeks up the signs of joint and simultaneously work; questioning about the steps of the production processes.

The complexity leads to the theme of Exchange's Need.

## 1.3 Exchange's Needs.

The former two items that define the networks lead to the necessity of exchanges. Having interdependence and complexity of tasks, participants find themselves on the need for exchanges, even if this refers to resources which are strategic, such as production processes, expertise, and availability of human resources.

What happens is that working together requires knowing the skills of some and being shared by others to improve processes; therefore, the deficiencies or weaknesses must be known also for process improvement. Thus, if a bank manager has data on the demand for withdrawals over the weekend, he should talk to other organizations, which have their specialties, to plan the supply for this demand.

When organizations are similar, as in the case of a group of strawberry growers; exchanges are regarding to specific knowledge of common domain and must be transferred to others to reduce differences in quality, times and other issues.

In short, the network format requires the exchange of experiences, which only occurs if there is a disposal for collective action.

## 1.4 Awareness of the need for collective action

Despite the organizational environment change in the sense of complexity and need for collective actions, the mindset of the lone entrepreneur when competing with others is very strong. This is evidenced in studies and consultancies, as well as in meetings with representatives of institutions, including government and supporting organizations such as banks, universities and research institutes. We have seen the strong presence of the particular advantage model, repeated several times in the question *"... but what do I get with that?"*

Awareness of collective action is a mindset (an attitude, in the old concept) of having to perform collective tasks (such as the exchange of information,) in a matrix of reasoning that can unite the result of collective action with the particular advantages. As mindset, it needs to be built from the social relations (that repeat this ethic or value), and from facts (such as the critical situation of the company). The consciousness of collective action is manifested in the signals of commitment, reciprocity and lack of opportunism.

Research on awareness of collective action can be performed directly questioning people from a group of organizations, or participating in meetings (if any), seeking for signs of disposal to act together and put their resources to collective use.

The awareness of collective action is enhanced when there are collective objectives.

## 1.5 Collective objectives existence.

Every kind of business presents some problems that affect all organizations that are in its field, which can lead to actions to gather with the purpose of discussing and solving these common problems. When they become critical (for example, new legislation that creates barriers to business), there is a strong collective goal that drives the efforts of participants, decreases the differences and competition among them (at least while the problem is addressed), and it places the need for collective action above those particular ones.

When the issue that generated the collective goal is quickly remedied, companies can return to its normal routine of competition. However, when the problem is more permanent and requires a change in the operation mode (for example, a new technology that threatens the product), then the possibilities for a group in network format arise, aided by the force of collective goals.

The investigation of the collective objectives searches for what problems are common to companies of that business, and questions about how they are trying to solve these common problems.

This common problems solution can pass through the presence of group rules.

## 1.6 Presence of joint action rules.

One of the strongest signs of the network format is the existence of some agreements, rules and standards of joint action. If organizations have a minimum of collective effort to solve a common problem and get a collective objective, a minimum of incentive and control rules about the participants must be necessarily present. How do we do this together? Governance is the answer.

When governance emerges from the group itself, we consider that provisions, rules, and standards for joint action would arise in the meetings. The more clear and organized the rules are, the more established the ties and commitments are to collective action, and the more it inhibits opportunistic behavior.

The investigation of governance, where there is a formal or informal set of rules, is done with questions related to what should be done in the group, who participates, what is forbidden. That is, a line that question whether there are collective rules, what its nature is (if strictly commercial to cover ethical issues), and what its objective is (if it's to control or have incentive rules, such as gifts premiums and benefits for those who participate).

Table 1.1 summarizes the categories and the guiding concept for the construction of questions in collection instruments.

Table 1.1. The categories that characterize the network format.

| Category | Central concept | Research actions |
|---|---|---|
| 1.Interdependence | Specialization of tasks leads to the need for joint action | Search for examples of situations where the organization needs other to accomplish its tasks |
| 2. Complexity | The requirement of numerous, simultaneous and special tasks requires the participation of various organizations | Search for examples of cases where there is an evident need for joint action |
| 3. Exchanges need | The production requires the exchange of information between organizations | Search for information sharing examples, needed for production |
| 4. Awareness of the need for collective action. | A cooperative attitude is a prerequisite for the realization of joint actions | Investigate the attitudes and values of the actors about working together |
| 5. Existence of collective objectives | One problem, or common goal that adds efforts. | Research if there is any, and what the collective objectives of the group are |
| 6. Presence of joint action rules | Formal and informal rules that organize and control actions | Investigate the presence of inclusion and exclusion rules, defined roles and sanctions. |

These six categories, when united, characterize the network format and distinguish the group of participant relationships from other relationships, more characteristics of the market format or hierarchy. From the characterization of a network (which is the first step in an investigation of networks), there unfolds a range of research topics. Some, like innovation, power and commitment, will be presented in this book.

Despite the convergence on what characterizes a network, theories, models and assertions constitute a wide range.

## 1.7. About the range of paradigms, theories, models and methods of research on networks.

As Nohria and Eccles (1992) state, the network phenomenon has been explained from the various organizational theories. There are explanations from rational and economic theories, with topics such as advantages of obtained cost if the company is on the network; from social theories, with topics such as trust, commitment and governance in relations; from explanatory models of a new network society, in which all organizations are connected, whether they use or not their connections; from institutional theories, with topics such as legitimacy of partnerships and learning processes in the network; from game theory with topics such as reciprocity in relationships. For our purposes and location of the examples of the later chapters, we will comment on three approaches more often found in studies on networks.

### 1.7.1. The rational and economical approach.

In the rational and economical approach, the central idea is that the networks are competitive responses from companies, seeking better market positions. There is a rational decision of the businessman to enter, or not, a network of companies, according to their analysis of the costs and resources involved and the possible advantages to be gained. Articles in that line, as in Ebers and Jarillo (1998), do not deny the social and institutional aspects of the networks, but they are more focused on competitiveness indicators in the market to build their conclusions. One of the research themes in this economic rational line is the competition concepts, which claim the need to analyze and compare individual companies with each other. In this case, relations between the parties are placed as possible actions and not as basic features, which create questions about the ability of the rational and economic paradigm to capture the network phenomenon, as there is evidence that some resources and competitive advantages are born from the collective, as found in articles that use the term Social Capital (Dasgupta; Serageldin, 1999). Topics such as costs, market outcomes, acquired knowledge and governance are frequent in the researches following the rational and economic paradigm.

### 1.7.2. The social approach.

The basic statement of this approach is that social relations are a kind of background to guide the processes and the behavior of the network actors. A reference author is Granovetter (1985), whose concept of *embeddedness* refers to the inseparability of social and economic relations, noting that the economic and technological factors are immersed in social relations and influenced by them.

In other words, the actors are immersed in the network with different degrees of strength and nature. Some direct all its efforts to collectively act and participate in the network, both in the commercial as social nature; while others may have weaker connections, possible with enough to continue participation in the group. In strong ties there is greater proximity between people, that is, more frequent interactions and the creation of repetitive flows. On weak ties, the relationships are less repetitive, the frequency is not constant and the nature of exchanges is more commercial or technical.

The concept of immersion is associated with opportunism. The more committed the actor is on the network, he or she will be less likely to behave opportunistically, which is putting personal goals above the collective.

### 1.7.3. The approach of the networked society

The approach of the networked society values and affirms the existence of a new social structure based on networks, with technology as instrumental base. Sociology theories of large groups and communication theories form basis for articles and recurring topics, such as studies of social networks on the internet.

The philosophy of the networked society means that we are all interconnected with strong or weak ties; with different kinds of connections, whether economic, social, or political and this web of ties is what we call the network. As business (and society) are configured in the network format, the difference between groups of companies working together would be in an organizational state of those six categories that characterize the network format. In the combination of categories different states or network configurations arise.

The theoretical arguments of the networked society are based on authors often cited in the literature, as Granovetter (1985), Nohria and Eccles (1992), Uzzi (1997) and Castells (1999). The common general principle to the authors is that every company is networked, whether or not aware of the situation, either using or not its connections. The conjunction point for the formation of *ties* is interdependence, which means the need for organizations to act together, because when isolated they lack of the resources and they cannot perform all tasks.

A methodological advantage of this approach, in its principle that all organizations are networked, is the ability to choose any company to a research, regardless of signs of belonging to a formalized network.

Within these three approaches, there are various theories and network representation models, at a moment in which the structure is valued, in another dynamic, evolutionary stages and organization states. Despite this range, which shows a pre-paradigmatic field (Kuhn, 1996), academic research shows convergence as to the characteristic of the network phenomenon, accepting that they are complex formations with inseparable elements, with unstable and unpredictable relations with changeable settings according to the dominance and combination of the six categories that define the network format.

Table 1.2. shows the basic information about the three paradigms.

**Table 1.2. Comparison of the principles of the three paradigms of networks.**

| Paradigm → Category ↓ | Rational and Economic | Social | Networked Society |
|---|---|---|---|
| Basic Affirmation on networks | The network is formed because of motives and objectives of economic resources dependency. | The network is formed and developed from social relations; each actor is immersed and committed on the network. | All organizations are networked, whether or they are conscious or not about it; whether they use their connections or not. |
| Examples of theories and most referenced authors | Transaction costs (Williamson, 1981). Rational choices (Clemen, 1996). Game Theory (Axelrod, 1986). | Dynamic of small groups (Golembiewski, 1962). Communication Theory (Bitti, Zani, 1993). *Embeddedness* (Polanyi, Arensberg and Pearson 1957; Granovetter, 1985) | Sociology of large groups (Castells, 2000). Communication Theory (Bitti, Zani, 1993). Ecology (Maturana, Varela, 1995). Rhizome Theory (Deleuze, Guattari, 2000) |

| Most frequent object of study | Economic and resource variations in the network. | Social relations in the network. | Flow between the actors of the network. |
|---|---|---|---|
| More frequent research objectives | Relate the economic variable to other variables such as innovation and learning. | Verify how specific social issues, such as trust, affect the structure and dynamics of networks. | Describe processes of social and economic flows of networks in any state or stage of development. |
| Dominant research methodology | Positivist, seeking causal relationships. | Interpretive, phenomenological, searching for relationships between variables and between structure and dynamics. | Systemic models, creating system designs (networks) as specific objective. |
| Dominant research type | Quantitative, with hypothesis test. | Quantitative, with correlation tests. Qualitative descriptive and interpretive. | Qualitative, descriptive, historicist and interpretative. |
| General line of argument in the conclusions | Discuss the laws that determine the relationships between economic variables and others, such as the number of participants. | Discuss and advocate the importance of social issues, such as commitment, in trade relations. | Describe the organization and development state of networks, considering from latent states, to formally existing networks. |

As can be seen, there is wide variety of theories and their consequent methodologies. In the following chapters we present some examples of research topics, with its theoretical basis and specific research designs. They are examples that show the line of investigation of the researchers on networks of the Master's Program in Business Administration from the Universidade Paulista-UNIP.

Chapter 2 discusses the variable power in the formation, structure and dynamics of the networks. There is an important explanation to start with this theme. It occurs that power is the key variable, however it's been forgotten in theories, models and research on networks. An extensive literature search and a research with a group of business men in the food industry concluded on the urgent need to incorporate the power into major topics and debates about networks.

Chapter 3 develops the discussion of governance from the rational and economic perspective. Several authors and researchers say that governance is the most central and defining category of the networks. In this chapter the authors develop the concept of governance in supply chains, presenting a research model and the example of the Brazilian aircraft maintenance industry. This example clearly illustrates the participation of multiple stakeholders, regulatory agencies, airlines, manufacturers, maintenance shops and parts and materials suppliers, which form a large network with interdependence and with the necessary presence of formal and informal instruments of governance.

Chapter 4 analyzes the social bases of the processes in networks. The social approach is getting more and more space and legitimacy in the study of networks, incorporating knowledge of the Small Group Sociology, the dynamics of groups from the Social Psychology and studies of roles and rituals of Anthropology. A survey of small producers in the north of the Paraná state, in Brazil, was conducted. They showed strong signs of social rituals allied to business processes. In fact, the text presents convincing arguments about the social relations being the basis of business processes and network development.

The four chapters will discuss the bases of the networks, focusing on power, governance and social relations approach. Chapter 5 starts another part of the book consisting of the discussion of special topics such as innovation, learning and strategy.

In chapter 5 the authors propose to build an interface between the social network approach and relationship marketing, in search of better market results for companies. To bridge these two fields the authors studied common and complementary categories of relationship marketing and of the social approach of networks. These theoretical findings were then explored in the case of a famous ceramics company in Brazil that used relationship marketing techniques in a network context to recover from bankruptcy

Chapter 6 develops proposals for theoretical understanding and knowledge management mechanisms in networks. Items such as dissemination of knowledge, acquired memory and orientation to learn are placed in the perspective of network processes, that is, interdependence, complexity and need for exchanges with a social foundation of trust and cooperation. This is an important contribution to a topic rarely addressed in the network field.

In chapter 7 the authors discuss the interfaces between networks, innovation, and brand diffusion. Also, the areas of business and social network approach an interesting theoretical movement. How do companies place their brands on the social networks? What are the advantages and risks of this strategy? The authors compare the Harley-Davidson and Buell brands and their brand image aspect related to social networks as well as to innovations.

Chapter 8 shows the situation of social and commercial relations between organizations of the housing cooperative processes. The research achieved a result even somewhat surprising, because the organizations groups involved in the housing cooperatives are far from acting according to the principles of cooperativism, setting a format closer to the classical market competition, with price and product competition. The discussion shows that when certain environmental conditions become unfavorable each organization primarily seeks its survival in the market and loses his social objective.

Chapter 9 confers the challenges of conducting research on networks. The guiding idea is that the classical ways of data collection and interpretation, such as interviews and questionnaires, may be limited in their ability to capture the complexity and unpredictability of social, commercial and technical relations. In the chapter, a suggestion of a research design is presented, that could also be a guiding model for the planning and execution of research in the area.

# References.

Castells, M. The rise of network society. Cambridge: Willey Blackwell, v.1, 1999.

Cinner, J.; Bodin, O. Livelihood diversification in tropical coastal communities: a network-based approach to analyzing 'livelihood landscapes'. PLoS ONE, v.5, n.8, p.1-13, 2010.

Dasgupta, P.; Serageldin, I. Social capital: a multifaceted perspective. Washington: International Bank, 1999.

Dwyer, F.; Schurr, P. e Oh, S. Developing buyer-seller relationships. Journal of Marketing, v.51, n.2, p.11-27, 1987.

Ebers, M.; Jarillo, J. The construction, forms and consequences of industry networks. International Studies of Management and Organizations, v.27, n.4, winter, p.3-21, 1997/98.

Glasbergen, P. Global action networks: agents for collective action. Global Environmental Change-Human and Policy Dimensions, v.20, n.1, p.130-141, 2010.

Granovetter, M. Economic Action and Social Structure: The Problem of Embeddedness. The American Journal of Sociology, v.91, n.3, nov., p.481-510, 1985

Gulati, R. Alliances and networks. Strategic Management Journal, v.19, p.293–317, 1998.

Hakansson, H.; Snehota, I. Developing Relationships in Business Networks. London: T.J. Press, 1995.

Kuhn, T. 1970. The structure of scientific revolution. Chicago University, Chicago, IL, 37pp.

Nohria, N.; Ecles, R. Networks and organizations: Structure, form, and action. Boston: Harvard Business School, 1992.

Uzzi, B. (1997) Social structure and competition in interfirm networks: The paradox of embeddedness. Administrative Science Quarterly, 42(1), pp. 35-67.

# CHAPTER 2.

POWER: FUNDAMENTAL VARIABLE FORGOTTEN IN STUDIES
OF NETWORKS

Renato Telles
Walter Cardoso Sátyro

## 2. 1. Introduction

There is an increasing speed in the world changes, as stated by Meyer and Davis (1999), leading the company to a progressive and constant transformation. Adaptability has become vital, more than the development homeostasis skills, causing that a growing number of companies adopt strategies related to building networks, recognizing the fact of interdependence and the limited ability of a company to compete in isolation. According to Grandori and Soda (1995), the formation of these networks becomes increasingly frequent and relevant in economic life, for its ability to regulate the interdependent and complex transactions. Interdependent because the task of specialization creates the situation that needed resources are in domain of other organizations and vice versa, leading to joint work. Complex because production systems increasingly require joint and simultaneous action of various organizations for production, as in the financial system.

Organizations do not operate isolated, but in strategic alliances with other agents and organizations, including suppliers, customers and even competitors, involving exchanges, sharing and joint product development, technology or services (Gulati, 1998). A field of research relatively extensive and broad opened to the study of inter-organizational networks, particularly on understanding the governance of the operation of these joints, considering them as systems of cooperation and trust. The topic of power, however, it remained in the background, with comparatively fewer studies (Giglio; Pugliese; Silva, 2012; Krausz, 1988).

In the relationships among the members of networks, social exchanges occur including power relations (Krauz, 1988) as a natural and effective social phenomenon in the presence of interests (Dallari, 2013), or when there is conflict (Katz, Kahn, 1974). The Power in this sense is expressed as a relation, emerging from the need to organize and it seeks for the common good, or to assert its will in this social relationship (Chalita, 2005). According to Hughes and Appelbaum (1998), power and politics involve the organizations in a process of giving and receiving, without being possible to be disregarded. As Zaheer, Gözubüyük, and Milanov (2010), the power is one of the four theoretical mechanisms to the analysis of inter-organized networks and with no possibility of being ignored.

Network and power have been treated from different perspectives in various contexts. In a conjugated form, which means power in networks, the concept becomes important when considering the need for its understanding, keeping in mind its conditioning and determining aspect in the behavior of participant actors in the network and, as consequence, on its performance. The statement of a social background influencing the technical and commercial behavior of actors was presented and recognized some time ago (Granovetter, 1985; Gulati, 1998; Jones, Hesterly, Borgati, 1997), however, the power, as a dimension, category or context, is often not contemplated in studies and discussions on networks. A reason lies in the conception of these networks on interventions.

The notion of network is present in virtually all disciplines (Balestro, 2002), covering a range of meanings, from the fisherman's net, with its interwoven yarns, or the weaving networks forming fabrics that will dress the body, the networks of railways, networks of computers, networks of communication, crystal networks, immune networks, artificial neural networks, political networks, planetary networks, religious networks etc. (Musso, 2004). According to Nohria (1992), the companies are in network, using or do not using their connections, from conglomerates to small entrepreneurial companies. A firm cannot be separated or isolated from other relevant companies (Ho, 2006), enhancing the clustering process of these organizations in networks of companies, potentially more equipped for the competitive confrontation with different configurations of competition.

Among the benefits of this collective arrangement, it can be mentioned (1) the organization and regional development, (2) gained in learning through exchange of information, (3) development of new products and markets, and (4) ability to negotiate purchases (Balestrin; Vargas, 2004). Some of these benefits such as the ability to negotiate refer directly to a notion of power.

Power is a current topic in Philosophy, Sociology, Political Science, Psychology and Administration (Silva, 2007), with several approaches in function of theories used in each of these fields of knowledge (Giglio; Pugliesi; Silva, 2012). The word power derives etymologically from the Vulgar Latin *potere*, which replaced the classical Latin posse - meaning "being able" and "authority" (Silva, 2007; Ferreirinha; Raitz, 2010). The establishment of a typology of power is considered a task that involves difficulties (Dallari, 2013; Cecílio; Moreira, 2002), remaining as something undefined and difficult to be defined with precision (Chalita, 2005). The multiplicity of understandings about power derived from the variety of theoretical references different and no convergent (Cecilio; Moreira, 2002), together to the attraction that the power topic exercises in function of number of windows that it opens to the understanding of everyday life (Galbraith, 1999). Besides this range of concepts, power is also portrayed in numerous social, political, commercial and religious situations. It has, for example, research on (a) power of a parent over a child; (b) power of persuasion and seduction; (c) the power of the employer; (d) power of money; (e) three powers; and (f) power of God.

Thus, the central purpose of this chapter is the defense of a conceptual line of power that could be more competent to the research of networks. This line should be able to deal with the conceptual diversity and manifestations of the phenomenon, as well as defining and embracing the perspective (relations between actors, between the actor and the network, between networks), the context (features of the business and the game to keep, or get power), the perception of the actors (actor with power, actor without power) and the legitimacy of power on the considered group (power recognized and accepted, or not recognized and not accepted). A conceptual approach of power with that competence offers as epistemological advantage the consistency and adherent conception with the systemic and complex principles that define the networks, involving questions as self-organization, interdependence, evolutionary nature and solution of asymmetries.

Despite the diversity of the concepts of power, it is understood to be necessary and justified the effort to scan an adequate perspective and recognize capacity in the study of networks. The efforts of recognition and incorporation of power, as intrinsic and immanent dimension to the social relations, and as the development of a construct theoretically robust and operationally consistent, becomes a relevant demand in the research of inter-organizational networks. Thus, this study adopted as main objective the defense of a more competent concept of power for research of networks, from the published material analysis and reflections of the authors leading to a convergence.

## 2.2 Analysis Procedure

The investigation aimed to recognizing the theoretical bases to a proposition linked to a conceptual line of power to the study of networks, considering two perspectives of research:

(A) Power in organizations and networks from the classic literature, looking to critically inventory the cast of theoretical positions and potential convergences, recognizing the absence of philological concerns;

(B) Considerations about power from the panel of inventoried articles on the subject, involving networks.

### 2.2.1 Power in organizations and networks from the classical literature

There are two currents of reference about power in organizations, although none of them addresses frequently and clearly the collective relationships in business networks, according to Hardy and Clegg (2001):

**Critical perspective:** understanding topics and scopes as domination and exploitation, using statements of Marx and other social authors, seeking to explain and characterize the asymmetries between dominator and dominated.

**Functionalist perspective:** understanding issues associated to management objectives, using concepts of authority, leadership and persuasion as necessary to the management of a business.

According to Thorelli (1986), power, information, money and utilities flow along of the business networks, where the power is the central concept of network analysis due to its ability to influence the decisions or actions of others. The simple existence of power is enough to condition others. However, despite the power comes in with the idea of always being possessed unilaterally, the most typical power phenomenon is interdependence. Reading about business networks can give the impression that with the mastery of cooperation, competition would be with its days counted. But neither the competition nor the market can be neglected in studies of networks.

Stolte (1988), analyzing power in inter-organizational networks, defines power unbalance in a network when an actor is more dependent on the relationship with other than the reverse, which leaves one with disadvantage of power and the other with advantage. In this way, exchanges between actors become different, to the advantage of the actor with greater power. This unbalance or, in other words, asymmetry creates tensions in the way that the actors seek to return to equilibrium, where the exchange relationships can be balanced, to maintain their own formed business network

The comments of Thorelli (1986) and Stolte (1988) indicate that the possession can originate power, but the main manifestation of power is in the interdependence. Other authors also claim to the idea of power as relationship. According to Nohria (1992), studies of power in organizations have focused on aspects such as personality traits, formal position in the organization and control over resources. However, the author says business networks are socially constructed, reproduced and changed by the result of the actions of the actors, and despite that analysts of networks maintain that relationship patterns as stable and repetitive, they recognize that the bonds are constantly being rebuilt, implying recursively on reconfiguration of power relations, which modifies the structure and dynamics of the network. In other words, the power set the network.

This dynamic of the network and power relations is recognized by different authors (Kogut, 1989; Grandori; Soda, 1995; Gulati, 1998; Granovetter, 1985). The movement and the history of networks putting the power as a structuring factor in this dynamic process offer different perspectives of evolution and vitality to long of time.In this sense, according to some authors (M iles, Snow,

1984; Kogut, 1989; Granovetter, 1985). The power is so important that it can be responsible for the loss in competition and eventually collapse the network. A study developed by Park and Ungson (2001) on mortality rates of networks presents rates near to 50% to the investigated networks, with some of the cases explained by conflicts over power between the actors. According to Hakansson and Dubois (2002), in inter-organization network, both cooperation and the power are present, as though the relationships between organizations are cooperative in general, conflicts are inherent to the relationship.

The preceding paragraphs show that the authors accept and affirm the importance of the power construct in networks as a structuring factor. However, some of them (Nohria, 1992; Powell, 1990) defend, even that the network is defined by relations of power, and, classical concepts of power as a personal resource, or position in a hierarchy, are not enough to contemplate the analysis of the networks´ complexity.

This line of thinking builds an alternative route to the dominant models, that can be traced in Foucault's work (2002), which puts the power as routine, frequent relation, founder of the same company (therefore different from the personnel resource, or position in a hierarchy). Other concepts to the power can be retrieved: Parsons (1968) with the concept of systemic power, Luhmann (1983) with the concept of power as a agglutinator of groups, Mauss (1974) with the concept of power and grace, and Powell (1990) with the concept of governance and power. All of them follow this trail of power as something inherent to the relations between people. This conceptual line seems to be closer to the network phenomenon, where the present asymmetries put the actors in a situation permanently mediated and inseparable of relations of power.

Nowadays, the research of Zaheer, Gözubüyük and Milanov (2010) follows this path to put the power as an inherent relation to networks, immanent to the connections between actors. To the authors, the networks are configured on four pillars: access to resources, trust, power and signaling, which will be detailed later. It suppresses the power of the analysis of networks, implying reduction of understanding of the phenomenon. It offers power as one of the networks supporting bases, following the conceptual line of Foucault (2002), among others, setting the statement that the power in networks is an inherent phenomenon underlying and founding of the group itself. It is understood a conceptual line more competent to analyze the networks rather than the critical and functional approaches.

When the conceptual line is established sustaining power as a daily and inseparable relationship to networks, the second research task was developed. It consists on the analytical examination of manifestations of power in networks from panel of national and international recent articles.

## 2.2.2 Power from the panel of articles on power and networks

A research from the SciELO database - *Scientific Electronic Library Online* was held using the words power and networks, together on the search bar, associating all indexes (year, abstract, author, financier, journal and title) in Portuguese, Spanish and English, from 1999 to 2014. Twenty one works were identified in a period of 15 years that treated power in inter-organized networks. This result suggests an important shortage of articles on the subject, leading to an understanding about the reduced attention given to power in studies about networks. The results of bibliographical analysis on networks (Amantino-de-Andrade, 2004; Pereira; Venturini; Wegner; Braga, 2010; Giglio; Pugliese; Silva, 2012; Oliveira; Sacomano Neto, 2014) indicate the dominance of topics of cooperation and exchange, while the topic of inter-organizational power is rarely examined, even when articles refer to conflicts of interest, knowledge protection or conflicts by differences in resources. The revisions refer to the primacy of an economic and rational view, with topics about resources, authority, relationships, positions market and, secondly, the power. Even in cases where power is considered to a certain point, its concept comes from a functional perspective. Expressions found as a consensus of ownership, ideological consensus, positive assessment and work coordination, reveal this management aspect.

In the classical structural approach on networks (Burt, 1976), it is assumed that the centrality of an actor is associated to a position of power. Cook, Emerson, Gillmore and Yamagishi (1983) conducted empirical studies and computer simulations, showing that the centrality on business networks does not necessarily imply the power on the network. This result indicates that power is not necessarily linked to the centrality, but it could be associated with connectivity (Arten, 2013).

Based on the empirical results shown with the works of Cook et al. (1983) and his confrontation with the existing theory, Bonacich (1987) proposes that the centrality should also be a function of β, defined this as a parameter that reflects the degree to which the status of the individual says with respect to whom it is connected. Nevertheless, Bonacich (1987) recognizes that the model ignores all aspects affecting the centrality, the power of the units connected in the network, positively or negatively, citing the case of the model not reflecting the communications links with individuals outside the network, nor the differences in the quality of information received. The author concludes there are different types of centrality, depending on the degree of analysis, and there are occasions where the power is increased by association with others powerful, because it becomes part of a network with power status. There are cases where the power is increased to be part of a network with others of less power, citing the example of a large organization that combines networking with other smaller organizations to take advantage of its size to impose supply conditions for the smaller to provide.

Pinto and Junqueira (2009, p.1096), analyzing the power concentration of managers of a non-profit network, to investigate whether the same could be correlated with the maintenance of the network structure. They affirm the importance of a core manager for the maintenance of the network, which centralizes power, "and this centrality of power comes from its ability to offer benefits of interest of each member," thus confirming the assertion of Coleman (1998), that "the power of an actor networked lies in its ability to control events that create value, or that may be of interest to others".

These considerations are particularly important as they indicate that the position of a person in the group does not directly implies power (which is contrary to the functionalist perspective), but the power is the result of developments and conditions underlying the relations of this central actor with other actors (closer to the relational concept of Foucault, 2002 and others). Those arguments support the work´s statement. One of the administration support fields, which provide effective bases of support for the purpose of this essay, is the Social Psychology when discussing power. According to Rodrigues (1998), two theories stand out, coming from the Social Psychology. One, the theory of social power contains elements of the critical approach and the functional approach of power, but in the end, as Silva (2007) states, the basis of power is always the asymmetrical relationship between people, where their origin may be the power of reward, coercion, reference and specialty, among others. The other theory of power, with more grip and functionality in the study of networks is the theory of social exchange. This approach considers the path of power as a daily relationship, and inextricably present in any link among actors, which means natural and potentially more coherent to the networks´ perspective.

The theory of social exchange was introduced by Homans (1958), defining it as the exchange of material and immaterial goods, such as approval and prestige symbols. The purpose of these social exchanges is to maximize benefits, such as financial advantages, *status,* companionship and support, among others; and minimize efforts associated to all and any social relationship, including financial costs, time, social factors, emotional and efforts made to keep the relationship. Thibaut and Kelley (1959) sought to explain how people make, preserve or break a relationship, where the social interactions are explained by results obtained by A or B, with the introduction of the concept of Comparative Level defined:

**CL = r - c**

where:

CL ....... Comparative level

r ......... rewards

c ......... costs

Like this, in every relationship, interaction between people, when A emits the behavior a1, in return B emits behavior b1, of this relationship between A and B we have:

1. A receives the reward $r_{1A}$ and costs $c_{1A}$.

2. B receives a reward $r_{1B}$ and the costs $c_{1B}$, when the behaviors a1 and $b_1$ are performed.

As A and B will have rewards and costs to maintain the relationship, they will analyze the obtained results in the relationship through comparative level (CL), where:

**(A) CL> 0 (positive):** the relationship level is satisfactory, with the rewards greater than the costs to stay on the relationship.

**(B) CL = 0 (Zero):** the level of satisfaction is neutral, with the rewards equal to costs.

**(C) CL < 0 (Negative):** the level of relationship is unsatisfactory, with the costs exceeding the rewards to stay in the relationship.

In parallel to the relationship, people are confronted with alternatives that arise from other relationships, analyzed the comparative level of alternatives (CL alt).

**Figure 2.1. - Comparative Level (CL) and Comparative Level of alternatives (CLalt) of Thibaut and Kelley (1959).**

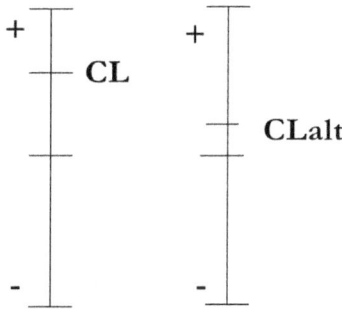

Source: Adapted from Rodrigues (1988).

Both the CL as CLalt are internal, subjective standards that also are influenced by the perception of every person in the analysis of alternatives that he or she would have available to compare with the current relationship, and consider its permanency, or exit. Thus, even with the comparative level (CL) negative, the person can stay in the relationship, because the comparative level of alternative (CLalt) which is presented is worse than the comparative level (CL) where he or she is; or the person remains in an unsatisfactory relationship, even though better alternatives, for personal considerations (Thibaut; Kelley, 1959). As Thibaut and Kelley (1959) relationship model, all relationships result in interactions where each person on the relationship has the possibility of affect the position of others, thus influencing or controlling the other. In every relationship each person has a certain ability to exercise power over another, classifying power in two:

**A. Power of destination control.** When A, by varying its behavior, affects the behavior of B, regardless of what B does, being this considered more a relationship of dependency.

**B. Power of behavior control.** When A, by varying its behavior makes it desirable to B to vary its behavior also, in this case it is considered more a relationship of interdependence, suggesting natural considerations of situations of cooperation and competition.

While the power of destiny results from a dependent relationship of B on A, for example, a company A asks to its supplier B to cut its prices, or it would buy raw material from another competitor, this will affect the behavior of B somehow, so as to continue to provide B will need to be positioned at the customer A demand.

But the power of behavior control results from an interaction effect that can cause interference, or facilities that reduce or increase the rewards of B. That would be the case of company A presenting good results by following a particular administrative practice, and B ends up adopting the same practice.

This also opens up the possibility to a third classification of power, where both A and B can exercise power over each other, as in every relationship there is interdependence between the parties (Thibaut; Kelley, 1959).

Concluding the discussion on this item 2, it was placed at the beginning the defense of the conceptual line of power as one of the bases that sustain the networks. The analysis of the statements of classical authors showed the presence of power approaches, critical and functionalist ones, which were considered insufficient to network analysis. The selection of a panel of more contemporary articles including other support areas of administration, confirmed the tendency to define power as immanent and inherent in social relations, including the network relations.

## 2.3. Concept line of Power for Networks.

As stated in the previous paragraphs there is an alternative pathway of definition of power that is different from the dominant approaches. Foucault (2002) places the power as a routine, frequent routine, creator of the society itself, so different from the approach of power as a personal resource, or due to a position in a hierarchy; Parsons (1968) with the concept of systemic power; Luhmann (1983) with the concept of power as an agglutinator of groups; Mauss (1974) with the concept of power and grace and Powell (1990) with the concept of governance and power, understanding this trail of power as something inherent to the relationship between persons, a conceptual line that appears closer to the networks phenomenon.

Table 2.1. presents the concepts and authors that converge in the affirmation of power being inherent in the relationship between organizations. Over the last reference to Table 2.1., Zaheer, Gözubüyük and Milanov (2010) must be recognized the differential contribution of content, by the currency of work and their power perspective as a structuring of networks. The authors suggest consideration of the following concepts in the capture and operationalization of the dimensions and variables present in its model:

(1) **Ego:** it refers to the actor in focus (the organization or firm);

(2) **Alter:** it refers to the actors (organizations or firms);

(3) **Access to resources:** the networks are usually studied as important sources or resources and capabilities. The resources can have origins in the relationship features, being the information one of the most cited in studies;

(4) **Trust:** networks generate trust, as organizations are more connected with each other, which would be associated with the reduction of opportunism and cost transaction;

(5) **Power and control:** networks restrict how much the actors' power increase. Studies analyzing dependency from one or more organizations of resources supplied by others, so that they would have more power, until

network formation, as a coalition between organizations to face another more powerful;

**(6) Signaling:** networks also act as signals in the market, where the quality of an actor can be inferred by the level of relationship he has, especially when there is difficulty in this measurement by direct way.

Table 2.1. - Approaches of Power on networks

| CONCEPT OF POWER | BASIC IDEA | AUTHORS |
|---|---|---|
| **As a collective end** | Actors that come from a given community must perform legitimate actions by the community | Parson |
| **As collective exchanges** | Circulation of material goods, in collectivity, lived under the sign of spontaneity | Mauss |
| **As agglutinator of groups** | The power groups the individuals, by their position of communication media in their social interactions | Luhmann |
| **As interdependence** | The power as the basis for regulation of relations between the actors of the networks - formal and informal governance | Powell |

| | | |
|---|---|---|
| **As exercise** | The power manifests/occurs itself associated to the relations, regardless of the possession or legitimacy | Foucault |
| **As one of the bases of networks** | Variable conditioned to the decision at an analysis level to be adopted in the research (Dyad, ego or network) | Zaheer, and Gözubuyuk Milanov |

**Source: Adapted from Giglio, Pugliese, and Silva (2012).**

Table 2.2 presents the four categories and the level of analysis in network research. This conceptual line of power called theory of social exchange is about the interaction between individuals (Thibaut; Kelley, 1959), about being able to cover the interdependence, which is one of the basic manifestations of networks. Interdependence places the actors immediately in a relationship of power, when it is considered that the exchanges are required. This game of power in both ways follows the trail of the statements of Foucault (2002) and others, culminating in the statements of Zaheer, Gözubüyük, and Milanov (2010), placing power as a pillar of networks.

Table 2.2. - Theoretical mechanisms in the network and theoretical developments approach

| THEORETICAL MECHANISM | LEVEL OF ANALYSIS | | |
|---|---|---|---|
| | Dyad - Relationship between two actors | Ego - Relationship of the actor with group | Network - Relations between all actors |
| ACCESS TO RESOURCES | Strong and weak ties determining knowledge transfer | Centralization determining access to information, skills and learning | Networks generating effective transfer of knowledge and regional success |
| TRUST | Strong ties increase trust and performance | More closed centrality and networks | The networks increase the regional success |
| POWER | Asymmetries and dependencies create ties and restrictions of interest | Power of subject position according to its ties | Networks create strategic blocks (power of competition) |
| SIGNS | Signs of trust and power in relations | Centralization resulting in power and status | Internal and external signals indicating power and trust on the network |

Source: Adapted from Zaheer, Gözübüyük and Milanov (2010) and Giglio, Pugliese, and Silva (2012).

Considering the rarity of what it is mentioned about power in networks following this trail, the following paradigm is formulated:

Power is an underlying attribute to the relationship, perceived by the actors as a result between benefits and efforts in this interdependence condition, resulting in ultimately, in conscious processes of submission, by influence or control, conditioned to reduce uncertainties and risks.

Within this conceptual line power there is a social phenomenon, present in social relations in the networks, and necessary for asymmetries resolution process of any nature.

## 2.4 Implications

Accepting the paradigm of power as underlying to the relationship, with a structuring nature of the group, according to the proposition, some theoretical and methodological implications resulting from this position are presented.

### 2.4.1 Theoretical Implications

One of the developments that can be understood as an advance or theoretical benefit is the convergence, compatibility and suitability from a dynamic and evolutionary perspective of networks, and a concept of power immanent and inseparable of social relations. When power is conceptualized, an internal logic between the statements, necessary condition (though not sufficient) for the validity of a concept is obtained.

Another important result is the increase in value of power as a structure of the configuration of networks, which it is rarely observed within their work. In most studies involving power, the use of functionalist concepts prevails as perspective, or even the association with personal resources. This has proven unsuitability in understanding networks, particularly by offering a potentially reductionist perspective of the phenomena. The inclusion of power as immanent relationship of networks embraces the possibilities of research conflicts, asymmetries, games of interest, defined as problems when using classical notions networks. In the proposed conceptual approach, these issues do not show problems, but the essence of the dynamics of network

## 2.4.2. Methodological implications

A natural deployment on the methodological dimension of the proposition of this work is the decision by the incorporation of the construct power in research networks. In other words, studies rejecting the consideration of power as structuring networks or treating power according to critical or functionalist approaches should deserve reservations when considering and interpreting their results. Another Methodological implication, of a more operational character, is the need to develop instruments and capture metrics of that variable.

## 2.5 Final Thoughts

The purpose of this chapter is to present a conceptual line proposal on networks that were more competent to investigate this phenomenon, than the dominant approaches. There are two dominant approaches that agglutinate the many concepts of power in the organizations including the networks format. The first approach, called Critical consists of the definitions of power as domination, from the possession, or position of Classic Sociology works, as Marx's texts, analyzed by Buey (2007), are widely used in this approach. The second approach, called Functionalist, consists in the definition of power as favorable situation for behavioral changes in others. Classic Psychology studies on leadership and authority are widely used in this approach.

When considering the convergence of the idea of network, it is clear that none of them have enough competence to understand the power in networks. If the networks are defined as collective actions based on the existence of interdependence, an organizational environment where competition is being improved between groups, then it would have the possession (critical approach), or a position in an organization (functional approach). It does not imply in solution of the interdependence, which is the first collective goal of a network.

From these reflections, the defense of a third way of understanding power is set up, traced in earlier works of Foucault (2002) and others, in which power is placed as a routine in social relations of any kind, including commercial relations. Therefore, power is considered the founding element of the group, which means, an uplifting/structuring element of the network, whatever its nature is. In other words, in the networks language, the search for solution of asymmetries between the actors of a network, manifested by differences in resources of all kinds, is what gives standard and consistency to the photography (structure, dynamics and operation) of that specific network. The power portrays the network.

One of the consequences of the acceptance of this proposition is that the studies on networks would incorporate, as routine the variable power, as it involves the interdependence or cooperation.

# References

Amantino-de-Andrade, Jackeline. Actor-network theory (ANT): uma tradução para compreender o relacional e o estrutural nas redes interorganizacionais? Cadernos EBAPE.BR, Rio de Janeiro, v. 2, n. 2, jul. 2004, p. 1-14.

Appelbaum, S. H.; Hughes, B. Ingratiation as a political tactic: effects within the Organization. Management Decision. 36/2, 1998. p. 85-95.

Arten, F. T. Inovatividade em clusters de negócios comerciais: um estudo sobre a relação entre a capacidade de inovação e a estrutura das redes sociais presentes nas redes de negócios. 2013. 109 f. Dissertação (Mestrado em Administração).– Universidade Paulista, São Paulo. 2013.

Balestrin, A.; Vargas, L. M. A dimensão estratégica das redes horizontais de PMEs: Teorizações e evidências. RAC, ed. especial, 2004, p. 203-227.

Balestro, M. V. Confiança em rede: a experiência da rede de estofadores do pólo moveleiro de Bento Gonçalves. 2002. 118 f. Dissertação (Mestrado) – Universidade Federal do Rio Grande do Sul, Porto Alegre, 2002.

Bonacich P. Power and Centrality: A Family of Measures. American Journal of Sociology, v. 92, n. 5, mar. 1987. p. 1170-1182.

Buey, F. F. Marx e os marxismos. Uma reflexão para o século XXI. In: Boron, A. A.; Amadeo, J.; Gonzalez, S. A teoria marxista hoje: problemas e perspectivas, 2007. Disponível em: http://bibliotecavirtual.clacso.org.ar/ar/libros/campus/marxispt /cap. 7.doc>. Acesso em 16 nov. 2013.

Burt, R. S. Positions in Networks. Oxford University Press. v.55, n.1, 1976. p. 93-122.

Cecílio, L.; Moreira, M. E. Disputa de interesses, mecanismos de controle e conflitos: a trama do poder nas organizações de saúde. Revista de Administração Pública – RAP/ EBAPE / FGV. Rio de Janeiro 36 (4) jul. / ago 2002. p. 587-608.

Chalita, G. O poder. Reflexões sobre Maquiavel e Ettiénne de La Boétie – 3.ed. ver. – São Paulo: Editora Revista dos Tribunais, 2005.

Coleman, J. S. Foundations of social theory. Cambridge: Harvard University Press, 1998. Disponível em: http://books.google.com. br/books?hl=pt-BR&lr=&id=a4Dl8tiX4b8C&oi=fnd&pg=PR15& dq=foundation+of+social+theory&ots=qCZqU-NZFj&sig=Md9Y csSYjL8qtdReQgD9tUFVrrg#v=onepage&q=power&f=false. Acesso em: 29 mai. 2014.

Cook, K. S.; Emerson, R. M., Gillmore, M. R., Yamagishi, T. The Distribution of

Power in Exchange Networks: Theory and Experimental Results. The American Journal of Sociology, v. 89, n. 2, set., 1983. p. 275-305.

Dallari, D. A. Elementos de teoria geral do Estado. 32. ed. São Paulo: Saraiva, 2013.

Dubois, A.; Hakansson, H. Relationships and activity links. In: EBERS, M. The formation of inter-organizational networks. New York: Oxford University Press, 1. reimp., 2002.

Ferreirinha, I. M. N.; Raitz, T. R. As relações de poder em Michel Foucault: reflexões teóricas. Revista de Administração Pública – RAP, 44(2), Rio de Janeiro, 2010, p. 367-383.

Foucault, M. Microfísica do poder. 17. ed. Rio de Janeiro: Graal, 2002.

Galbraith, J.K. Anatomia do poder. 4. ed. São Paulo: Pioneira, 1999.

Georgia, N. Positivismo – Conceito e resumo de suas características. Disponível em: < http://www.estudopratico.com.br/positivismo-conceito-e-resumo-de-suas-caracteristicas>. Acesso em: 07 jul. 2014.

Giglio, E.M.; Pugliese, L. R.; Silva, R. M. Análise dos conceitos de poder nos artigos brasileiros sobre redes. Revista de Administração da UNIMEP. v.10, n.3, set/out, 2012.

Grandori, A.; Soda, G. Inter-firm networks: antecedents, mechanisms and forms.

Organization Studies. Viena, v. 16, n.2, 1995. p. 183-214.

Granovetter, M. Economic action and social structure: the problem of embeddedness. The American Journal of Sociology, Chicago, v. 91, n.3, nov. 1985, p. 481-510.

Gulati, R. Alliances and Networks. Strategic Management Journal, v. 19, n. 4, Special Issue: Editor's Choice. abr.1998, p. 293-317.

Hardy, C.; Clegg, S.R. Alguns ousam chama-lo de poder. In: CLEGG, S.R.; Hardy, C.; Nord, W.R.. Handbook de estudos organizacionais. São Paulo: Atlas, 2001, v. 2, p.260- 289.

Ho, C.H. Exchange-based value creation system for networks relationships management. The Journal of American Academy of Business Cambridge. v.9, n.1, mar. 2006, p. 202-209.

Homans, G. C. Behavior as exchange. American Journal of Sociology, v. 63, n. 6, mai. 1958, p. 597-606.

Jones, C.; Hesterly, W. S.; Borgatti, S. P. A general theory of network governance: exchange conditions and social mechanisms. The Academy of Management Review, v. 22, n. 4, out., 1997, p.911-945.

Katz, D.; Kahn, R. Psicologia social das organizações. 2. ed. São Paulo: Atlas, 1974.

Kogut, B. The stability of joint ventures: reciprocity and competitive rivalry. The Journal of Industrial Economics, v. 38, n. 2, dez. 1989, p. 183-198.

Krausz, R. R. O poder nas organizações. São Paulo: Nobel, 1988.

Luhmann, N. Insistence on systems theory: Perspectives from Germany--an essay. social forces, v.61, n.4, 1983. p. 987-998.

Mauss, M. Ensaio sobre a dádiva. Forma e razão da troca nas sociedades arcaicas. In: Mauss, M. Sociologia e Antropologia. v. II. São Paulo: Edusp, 1974.

Meyer, C.; Davis, S. Blur – A velocidade da mudança na economia integrada. Campus: Rio de Janeiro, 1999.

Miles, R. E.; Snow, C. C. Fit, failure and the hall of fame. California management Review, v.26, n.3, 1984. p. 10-29.

Musso, P. A filosofia da rede. In Parente, A. (organizador) Tramas da rede: novas dimensões filosóficas. Porto Alegre: Sulina, 2004, cap. 1, p. 17-28.

Nohria, N. Is a network perspective a useful way of studying organizations? In Nohria, N.; Ecles, R. Networks and organizations: Structure, form, and action. Boston: Harvard Business School, 1992.

Oliveira, L.; Sacomano Neto, M. Relações de poder em redes de negócios: Um estudo bibliométrico a partir da Web of Science. SIMPOI, 2014.

Park, S.; Ungson, G. Interfirm Rivalry and Managerial Complexity: A Conceptual Framework of Alliance Failure. Organization Science v. 12, n. 1, 2001. p. 37-53.

Parsons, T. Uma visão geral. In: Parsons, T. (organizador) A sociologia americana: perspectivas, problemas, métodos. São Paulo: Cultrix, 1968.

Pereira, B.; Venturini, J.; Wegner, D.; Braga, A. Desistência da cooperação e encerramento de redes interorganizacionais: Em que momento essas abordagens se encontram? RAI – Revista de Administração e Inovação. v.7, n.1, 2010. p. 62-83.

Pinto, A.; Junqueira, L. Relações de poder em uma rede do terceiro setor: um estudo de caso. Revista de Administração Pública – RAP, 2009 p. 1091-1116.

Powell, W. Neither market nor hierarchy: Network forms of organization. In: B. Staw & L. L. Cummings (Eds.), Research in Organizational Behavior. Greenwich, CT: JAI Press. 1990: p. 295-336. Disponível em: < http://woodypowell.com/wp-content/uploads /2012/ 03/10_powell_neither.pdf>. Acesso em: 14 jan. 2014.

Rodrigues, A. Psicologia social. 17.ed. Petrópolis: Vozes, 1998.

Silva, C. O poder nas organizações: Um estudo preliminar a partir da percepção dos trabalhadores.2007. 256 f. Dissertação (Mestrado em Psicologia) – Instituto de Psicologia, Universidade Federal de Uberlândia, Uberlândia, 2007.

Stolte, J. From micro-to-micro-exchange structure: measuring power imbalance at the exchange network level. Social Psychology Quarterly. v. 51. n. 4.,1988, p. 357-364.

Thibaut, J.; Kelley, H. The social psychology of groups. New York: Wiley, 1959.

Thorelli, H. Networks: betweeen markets and hierarchies. Strategic Management Journal, v.7, n.1, jan./fev., 1986, p. 37-51.

Zaheer, A.; Gozubuyuk, R.; Milanov, H. It's the connections: the networks perspective in interorganizational research. The Academy of Management Perspectives, v.24, n.1, fev. 2010. p. 62-77.

# CHAPTER 3.

## RATIONAL VISION OF GOVERNANCE IN SUPPLY NETWORKS

Marcio Cardoso Machado,
Carlos Eduardo Santos,
Saturnina A. Martins

### 3.1. Introduction

The approach by networks can provide *insights* that other perspectives cannot achieve (Nohria and Eccles, 1992). According to the authors, from this perspective organizations can be classified as a network and thus are better understood. The change of an individualized analysis of companies for vision about the interactions between them became the basis for the business and academic thought in the 90s. The authors say that during this period the interest in the interactions, relationships and networks was developed more when the term "relationship marketing" was created, and it was also at this stage that more *insight into* interactions, relationships and networks were achieved (Ritter; Gemunden, 2003).The network approach advanced to many lines of discussion, for example, the global manufacturing operations that now deal with network providers or more precisely supply networks (Easley; Kleinberg, 2010).

The term *Supply Chain Management* originated in the early 1980s to describe the benefits from the integration of the internal functions of procurement, manufacturing, sales and distribution (Ballou; Gilbert; Mukherjee, 2000; Hakansson; Persson, 2004; Harland; Johnsen; Zheng, 2001). This approach focused on internal processes gave way to a broader idea of Supply Chain, when Jones and Riley (1985) defined it as an integrative approach to dealing with the planning and control of material flow from suppliers to consumers end.

The network approach applied to the Supply Chain arises in the 1990s, conceptualizing that it is a network of organizations that are involved upstream and downstream, by different processes and activities that produce value in the form of products and services for the end customer (Ellram, 1991;

Lee, NG, 1997; Lee; Billington 1992). So for a more realistic representation of supply chain management complexity becomes more appropriate to use the term network instead of chains (Burgess; Singh; Köroglu, 2006).

The supply chain is a network of organizations and for this reason should be considered from a perspective where the network is composed of nodes and *links,* where each node as an *agent* capable of making decisions and maximize its earnings within certain patterns in which it operates (eg: manufacturers, warehouses, logistics operators and financial institutions), and the *links* refer to the connections between nodes (Carter; Rogers; Choi, 2015). Such connections can generate, or not, collaboration among agents. The collaboration in supply chains emerges as an area of natural research due course of studies on integration and its direct impact on the performance of organizations (Cao; Zhang, 2011).

In the level of networks analysis in Supply Chain, relationships are identified not only among the companies that make up the direct supply chain, as well as relations in a wide range of organizations that somehow contribute to this chain (Miemczyk, Johnsen and Macquet, 2012). For Croom, Roman and Giannakis (2000), the relationships and existing partnerships in a supply chain can include: development of suppliers, strategic supplier selection, partnerships, involvement of suppliers, relationship marketing, supplier evaluation, etc. Therefore, it is necessary to understand how relationships and partnerships that exist in supply chains are extended to the network environment, which instruments are used to establish such relationships and what results can be achieved from these instruments.

According to Grandori and Soda (1995), the set of instruments that coordinate participating organizations from a network, in order to obtain certain result, is governance. Humphrey and Schmitz (2001) use the term governance to express that some firms in the chain create or force parameters under which the other participating companies must operate. A chain without governance becomes just a chain of market relations. Therefore, for the authors, the concept of governance within the global value chains is central.

Another frequently referenced article is that of Jones *et al.* (1997). In the model presented in this article, it is stated that governance is a system where, from meetings between the actors, own ways of interaction are established among them, making social ties clear , pointing greater security for relations on business. Repeated meetings will create a kind of group culture itself, with the emergence of some implicit rules, such as inclusion criteria and some rules may become explicit, such as signing a document for technological domain protection.

As these rules contribute to the solution of exchanges and collective action problems, it feeds back to a strengthening of social relationships circuit and therefore the strengthening and legitimacy of internal rules. Jones model values the governance that arises from group dynamics, be it of formal or informal nature.

Wind, Fung and Fung (2012) states that the networks need orchestration, and this consists in the company's design and management, that cooperate to achieve a common business process. Yet according to the authors, the success of a network depends on its project, processes and governance.

Even if governance tools (such as contracts, standards and social norms) have been identified, mainly from researches related to companies in dyads, their connections to specific results, taking into account different environments of supply networks, have not been studied systematically (Pilbeam; Alvarez; Wilson, 2012). Thus, the governance tools that support and sustain the cooperation and collaboration between the organizations participating in a supply network, for the achievement of common goals, may be different given a formal or informal governance.

As Richey *et al.* (2010), decision-makers have recognized the importance of supply chain management, mainly due to factors such as globalization, pressures on deadlines, quality expectations and market uncertainty. These factors point to the need to organize governance structures and activities to respond effectively and efficiently to global dynamics.

## 3. 2.Governance in Supply Networks

Research on governance in supply chains has become common topic and of great importance to understand the operations of supply chains dynamics (e.g.: Bitran; Gurumurthi; Sam, 2006; De Graeve, 2004; Dolci, 2011; Humphrey; Schmitz, 2001; Padovani, 2007; Pilbeam; Alvarez; Wilson, 2012).

According to Bitran, Gurumurthi and Sam (2006) there is a need for the existence of roles or responsible agents that enable coordination and governance of the various segments of the supply chain, to keep its objectives as a whole. Formal or informal governance tools assure the achievement of these objectives (results) and some mechanisms, such as: power, trust, competence, partnership and transaction costs facilitate the action of these instruments of governance (Pilbeam; Alvarez; Wilson, 2012).

Spina *et al.* (2013), in an extensive survey in publications on procurement and supply management, found that the "relationship" between the actors is one of the most searched topics. They divided the subject into three topics: *partnership*, the most popular and fastest to grow in the last decade; *trust*, which appears second in the wide number of articles on this subject, also with a significant growth in the same period . This might even have been considered a common topic in literature about negotiation, which the researched articles constantly allude to.

Pilbeam, Alvarez and Wilson (2012) argue that, for example, trust can be critical for organizations in uncertain environments, requiring agility and quick responses that are usually hampered by contractual governance instruments common in relationships where there is less confidence. Trust may be required also for the successful outcome of supply networks in high-risk scenarios.

Yet according to the authors, governance instruments, supported by contractual trust, cannot be sufficiently flexible to govern relations in environments with rapid change. Going beyond the formal instruments of governance can be difficult for companies in a globalized supply chain, where the possibilities for interaction and greater understanding of the behavior of another company are less likely than in regional supply networks or locations. So there are mechanisms that facilitate the governance instruments in regional or local supply networks which can provide important *insights* for understanding globalized scenarios.

To Neutzling and Nascimento (2013), supply chains are characterized by a high degree of interaction between organizations and the best way to manage sustainable supply chains is by combining appropriate governance mechanisms. Bellamy and Basole (2012) identified governance as one of the strategies to prepare and manage issues that emerge with the changes and evolution of supply chain networks.

Therefore, a rational and economic vision of governance in supply networks goes beyond the understanding of the informal aspects of governance relations, bringing to the context formal elements, such as standards, processes, structures and contracts.

### 3.2.1. Governance Analysis Method in Supply Networks

One way to understand the governance in supply networks from a more rational and economic vision is to use the method of Project of Propositions CIMO- *logic* treated by Denyer; Tranfield and Van Aken (2008).

### 3.2.1.1. Project of Propositions

The method of Project of Propositions comes from the initial idea that to achieve certain results (R), in a given context (C), one has to use the intervention type (I). Therefore, the key component will be the intervention type (I), used to solve the problem at hand, in this case governance tools. A Project of Propositions can be seen then as a model for creating solutions to a particular class of a larger field of problems. However, the authors, moved the initial idea and adapted this method for a contextual contingent structure, where the instruments of governance (I) can produce different Outcomes *(O)* (changed to results (R) in adaptation to Portuguese ) for the supply chain based on different mechanisms (M) depending on the specific context of the supply chain. To this new approach the authors have named CIMO- logic (Context, Intervention, Mechanism, Outcome - logic) (Denyer; Tranfield; Van Aken, 2008).

**The context (C)** relates to the internal or external environment in which the studied organization operates, as well as the characteristics of the actors participating in the supply chain, considering its history and types of partnerships.

**The Interventions (I)** are associated with the instruments of governance, formal or informal, which according to Pilbeam, Alvarez and Wilson (2012) enable the supply networks. These instruments support and sustain the cooperation and collaboration between the participating organizations of the supply network to achieve common goals. Understanding informal instruments those arising from immersion in a social structure and from the attention of the development of social norms that encourage or not the behavior at the organizational level as well as individually. And formal instruments are standards, processes, legal contracts, organizational or individual (functional) structures. Informal instruments can also compose the so-called relational governance and the formal instruments as contractual governance (Zhang; Aramyan, 2009).

**Mechanisms (M)** are the theories through which the instruments of governance will produce certain results (R). For this research project, the mechanisms *(theory)* for governance in supply networks were divided into four types (see: Dolci 2011, 2013; Rodriguez; Malo, 2006):

Agency Theory: According to this theory, shareholders and managers have conflicting interests, including with respect to risk. Governance in this case is a set of practices to ensure control of the high management, with the features: own interests, conflicting goals, bounded rationality, information asymmetry, efficiency, risk aversion and information as a commodity (Eisenhardt, 1989).

Theory of Transaction Costs: The company is seen as a governance structure that deals with uncertainty and costs, which are influenced by the human agent that has limited rationality and sense of opportunism. Reduced objectivity of people can take them to act on behalf of their own interest opposed to the benefits for company (Williamson, 1979).

Theory of Resource Dependence: Organizations depend on the relationship with the external environment to survive, where governance practices are to develop this relationship in order to get all the resources and information necessary and ensure the survival of the organization (Rodriguez; Malo, 2006) .

Theory of Stakeholders: Organizations serve the interests of various groups or individuals in society and not just to the shareholders and owners. Thus, governance emerges as a set of practices to meet and balance the interests of these multiple stakeholders (Freeman, 1986).

Dolci (2011) clarifies that the different theoretical concepts do not occur in isolation in the supply chain, and one of them can stand out in interorganizational relationships. This predominance can be influenced by different variables: the structure of the chain, the links between business, the type of transactions, the existence of a large company that has influence and power over the others, and the existence of formal or informal contracts based on trust and benevolence.

**Outcomes (O)** relate to everything that can be accessed over the network from governance. Pilbeam, Alvarez and Wilson (2012) identified seven categories of results: creativity, viability, control, coordination, performance, legitimacy and the specific results of each company in the network. However, for the purposes of this research project, it has been considered the results categorization model in supply network proposed by (Dolci, 2013), dividing them in financial and operational (Figure 3.1). Each variable for financial and operational classes were obtained from the literature review (Pilbeam; Alvarez; Wilson, 2012; De Graeve, 2004; Harland et al., 2004; Neutzling; Nascimento, 2013; Richey et al., 2010; Torres; Antonio; Cario, 2012; Zhang; Aramyan, 2009).

**Figure 3.1: Conceptual framework of how governance tools assure specific outcomes**

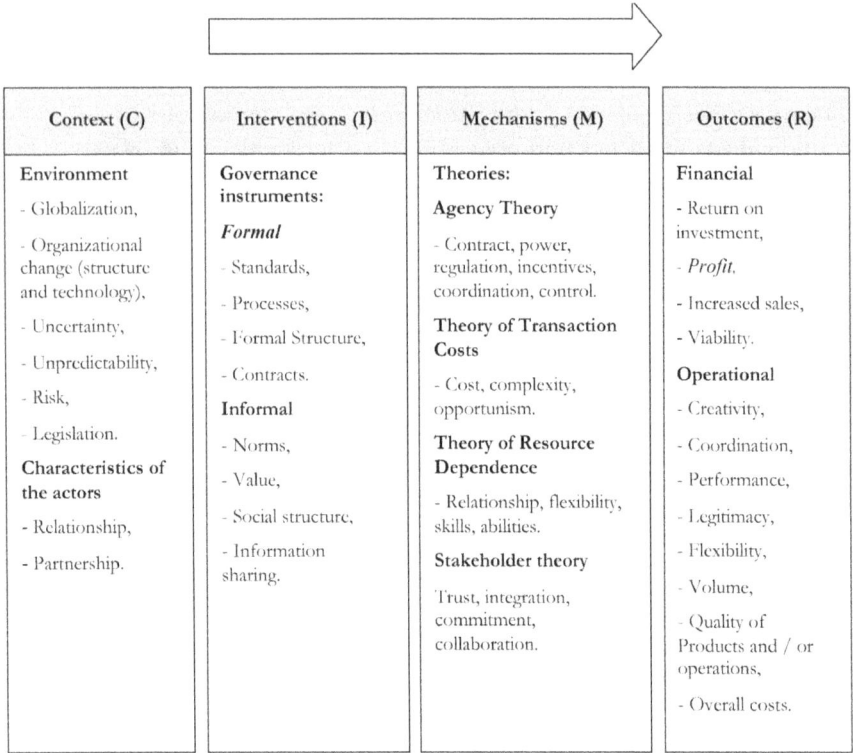

| Context (C) | Interventions (I) | Mechanisms (M) | Outcomes (R) |
|---|---|---|---|
| Environment | Governance instruments: | Theories: | Financial |
| - Globalization, | **Formal** | **Agency Theory** | - Return on investment, |
| - Organizational change (structure and technology), | - Standards, | - Contract, power, regulation, incentives, coordination, control. | - *Profit.* |
| - Uncertainty, | - Processes, | **Theory of Transaction Costs** | - Increased sales, |
| - Unpredictability, | - Formal Structure, | | - Viability. |
| - Risk, | - Contracts. | - Cost, complexity, opportunism. | **Operational** |
| - Legislation. | **Informal** | **Theory of Resource Dependence** | - Creativity, |
| **Characteristics of the actors** | - Norms, | | - Coordination, |
| - Relationship, | - Value, | - Relationship, flexibility, skills, abilities. | - Performance, |
| - Partnership. | - Social structure, | **Stakeholder theory** | - Legitimacy, |
| | - Information sharing. | Trust, integration, commitment, collaboration. | - Flexibility, |
| | | | - Volume, |
| | | | - Quality of Products and / or operations, |
| | | | - Overall costs. |

**Source: Adapted from Pilbeam, Alvarez and Wilson (2012)**

The Project of Proposition adapted by Pilbeam, Alvarez and Wilson (2012) received two contributions: the first was to synthesize the literature on governance in supply chains, given that few studies simultaneously treated the four components: context, intervention mechanisms and results. Thus enabling the development of three general Propositions:

*Proposition 1:* In case of change of organizational or technological structure, both formal and informal governance instruments are used to achieve viability, control, coordination and performance.

*Proposition 2:* In the circumstances of uncertainty / unpredictability or risk, formal governance tools provide an increase of viability, control, coordination and performance.

*Proposition 3:* Where there is an increased relationship between partners in the supply network, the adoption of informal governance tools can more easily lead to improvements in performance, control and viability.

The second contribution of Pilbeam, and Alvarez and Wilson (2012) is the actual research structure that can be used as a tool to analyze the governance supply networks. An adaptation of this structure can be seen in Figure 1.

Therefore, as shown in Figure 1, there are different variables that can be classified as a result of governance, aware of the impossibility of researching such a large number of variables, so we can infer that governance instruments affect the results of a network operations.

## 3.3. The case of governance in the supply network of aircraft maintenance companies

This section will apply the CIMO methodology to study the governance of the network of the Brazilian aircraft maintenance industry supplies.

### 3.3.1. The Context

In Brazil there are about five hundred maintenance workshops approved by the National Civil Aviation Agency (ANAC). These companies are located throughout the country, especially in the South and Southeast regions. These companies have the responsibility to return to service all aircraft equipment in need of repair or maintenance. And that means the existence of a network of parts supplies, materials and equipment that guarantee the perfect safety of aircraft.

According to data from 2007, from the Center for Research and Prevention of Aeronautical Accidents (CENIPA), about 20% of accidents involving civil aircraft has the maintenance of aeronautical materials as a contributing factor. Current data from the same agency showed no significant change in this scenario. This information reinforces the assumption of the need for greater understanding of maintenance activities undertaken by companies in the domestic airline industry, and the consequent flow of materials in the supply chain.

In view of the great demand for reliability in the services provided by suppliers, it is important to have in mind the need for understanding of governance mechanisms and their impact on guaranteed of desired results for the sector, namely: a high degree of aircraft availability, reliability of the maintenance and quality of parts used.

Figure 3.2 is a simplified way to network Brazilian aircraft maintenance, including aircraft maintenance repair stations (RS), regulatory agencies as the National Civil Aviation Agency (ANAC),, the North American agency *Federal Aviation Administration* (FAA) and the European Agency *European Aviation Safety Agency* (EASA) and the Airlines (C. Air). In this simplified representation of the supply network of the Brazilian aircraft maintenance industry (Figure 3.2), suppliers of maintenance workshops are not represented.

**Figure 3.2. Supply network representation of Brazilian aircraft maintenance industry.**

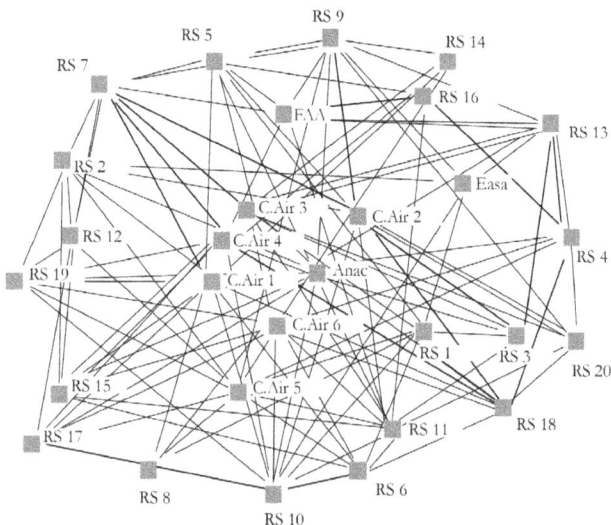

**Source: Authors**

### 3.3.2. Governance instruments in the Industry Supply Network Aircraft Maintenance

In the aircraft maintenance industry supply network there is a predominance of formal governance instruments. Figure 2 shows it is possible to see that the National Civil Aviation Agency (ANAC) has a higher degree of centrality and this, among other reasons, is because it plays a key role in the governance of the network. The main instruments of governance in the network are standards, processes and a formal framework based on international standards. It is possible to name a few instruments of governance: a maintenance workshop certification approved by ANAC, formal requirements that the maintenance shop needs to be able to join the network, contracts of the airline's maintenance workshops with such certification, invoices proving the origin of the maintenance workshops materials used and certified to ensure that these materials are also approved, or by the ANAC, or equivalent international bodies such as the FAA and EASA.

However, informal elements of governance are also present. The power of the manufacturers and the know-how guarantee offered by them ends up developing a kind of imposition for hiring their services. Another informal governance tool is the existing trust on information sharing relationships, given the need to rapidly disseminate data on possible problems in certain equipment operations, for companies that perform maintenance of such equipment can quickly incorporate changes needed in their processes and thus ensure the reliability of its operation.

### 3.3.3. Governance mechanisms in Industry Supply Network Aircraft Maintenance

Pertaining to governance mechanisms in the context of aircraft maintenance, organizations in this sector depend significantly on its relationship with the external environment, continually updating themselves with regard to new technologies incorporated in the aircraft, receiving real-time information on equipment malfunction, and also reliable suppliers of spare parts used in the maintenance process. These practices refer to the Theory of Resource Dependence.

It is also clear that these workshops are not exclusively linked to the dyads Workshops/Maintenance Airlines, there are also other actors who participate and have concerns about the results of these companies, such as: manufacturers of the aircrafts that do not want to see their products ( aircraft) involved in accidents; regulators, national (ANAC) and international (FAA and EASA) agencies who want to guarantee the airworthiness (safe flight); shareholders who seek positive financial results and passengers seeking reliable services. This conjunction of interests leads us to the Theory of *Stakeholders,* which appears as an important element in the governance of the network.

## 3.4. Results Obtained From Governance

Such instruments of governance, immersed in the particular context of the aircraft maintenance industry and supported by specific mechanisms, can lead to expected and necessary results for the sector. Financially, the return on investment and increase in profit, and operationally the quality assurance of offered service are examples of results. However, the principal among them is that a well-structured supply network can lead to guarantee, ultimately a safe flight.

## 3.5. Conclusion

From a rational and economic vision, governance in the supply network can play an important role in the results of certain companies. Depending on the type of industry and the context of its operations, the management of the flow of materials, from the manufacturer to the end customer served, can be a vitally important element in ensuring the desired performance.

The Brazilian aircraft maintenance industry exemplifies this more rational and economical approach. In its context, there is the participation of multiple players, regulatory agencies, airlines, manufacturers, maintenance shops and parts and materials suppliers, which form a large network. In this network, all depend on the various resources and all are imbued with a strong predisposition to ensure maximum safety and reliability of air transport operations. In this complex environment with multiple *stakeholders,* there are formal and informal instruments of governance, seeking to guide the actions of all involved to achieve common results. International rules and regulations unfold to the particular activities of each country and reflect throughout the supply network of the aircraft maintenance industry leading the reach of expected results.

Understanding how certain instruments of governance act for achieving certain goals can provide viability, control and reach the desired performance.

# References

BALLOU, R. H.; Gilbert, S. M.; Mukherjee, A. New Managerial Challenges from Supply Chain Opportunities. Industrial Marketing Management, v. 29, n. 1, p. 7–18, jan. 2000.

BELLAMY, M. A.; BASOLE, R. C. Network Analysis of Supply Chain Systems : A Systematic Review and Future Research. Systems Engineering, v. 16, n. 2, p. 235–249, 2012.

BITRAN, G. R.; GURUMURTHI, S.; SAM, S. L. Emerging Trends in Supply Chain Governance. Cambridge: [s.n.].

BURGESS, K.; SINGH, P. J.; KOROGLU, R. Supply chain management: a structured literature review and implications for future research. International Journal of Operations & Production Management, v. 26, n. 7, p. 703–729, 2006.

CAO, M.; ZHANG, Q. Supply chain collaboration: Impact on collaborative advantage and firm performance. Journal of Operations Management, v. 29, n. 3, p. 163–180, mar. 2011.

CARTER, C. R.; ROGERS, D. S.; CHOI, T. Y. Toward the theory of the supply chain. Journal of Supply Chain Management, v. 51, n. 2, p. 89–97, 2015.

CHANG, G. Total Quality Management in Supply Chain. International Business Research, v. 2, n. 2, p. 82–85, 2009.

CROOM, S.; ROMANO, P.; GIANNAKIS, M. Supply chain management: An analytical framework for critical literature review. European Journal of Purchasing and Supply Management, v. 6, n. 1, p. 67–83, mar. 2000.

DE GRAEVE, D. Framework for the study of governance in the supply networks Wal-Mart: the "Elightened Despot" model. [s.l.] Massachusetts Institute of Technology, 2004.

DENYER, D.; TRANFIELD, D.; VAN AKEN, J. E. Developing Design Propositions through Research Synthesis. Organization Studies, v. 29, n. 3, p. 393–413, 1 mar. 2008.

DOLCI, P. C. Um Modelo conceitual da Governança da Cadeia de Suprimentos: analisando suas concepções e elementos sob a ótica das teorias da governança.XXXV Encontro da ANPAD. Anais...Rio de Janeiro: 2011

DOLCI, P. C. Investimentos em TI, Governança da Cadeia de Suprimentos e Desempenho da Cadeia de Suprimentos: proposta de um modeloIV Encontro de Administração da Informação. Anais...Bento Gonçalves: 2013

EASLEY, D.; KLEINBERG, J. Networks, Crowds, and Markets: Reasoning About a Highly Connected World. [s.l.] Cambridge University Press, 2010.

EISENHARDT, K. M. Agency Theory: An Assessment and Review. Acad Manage Rev, v. 14, n. 1, p. 57–74, 1989.

ELLRAM, L. M. Supply-Chain Management: The Industrial Organisation Perspective. International Journal of Physical Distribution & Logistics Management, v. 21, n. 1, p. 13–22, 1991.

FERNANDES, A. C.; SAMPAIO, P.; CARVALHO, S. Quality Management and Supply Chain Management Integration : A Conceptual ModelInternational Conference on Industrial Engineering and Operations Management. Anais...2014

FREEMAN, R. E. Strategic Management: A stakeholder approach. Boston: Pitman, 1986.

GRANDORI, A.; SODA, G. Inter-firm Networks: Antecedents, Mechanisms and Forms. Organization Studies, v. 16, n. 2, p. 183–214, 1995.

HÅKANSSON, H.; PERSSON, G. Supply Chain Management: The Logic of Supply Chains and Networks. The International Journal of Logistics Management, v. 15, n. 1, p. 11–26, 2004.

HARLAND, C. et al. A Conceptual Model for Researching the Creation and Operation of Supply Networks. British Journal of Management, v. 15, n. 1, p. 1–21, mar. 2004.

HARLAND, C. M.; JOHNSEN, T. E.; ZHENG, J. A Taxonomy of Supply Networks. Journal of Supply Chain Management, v. 37, n. 3, p. 21–27, 2001.

HUMPHREY, J.; SCHMITZ, H. Governance in Global Value Chains. [s.l: s.n.].

JONES, C.; HESTERLY, W.; BORGATII, S. P. A general theory of network governance: exchange conditions and social mechanisms. The Academy of Management Review, v. 22, n. 4, out., 1997, p.911-945.

JONES, T. C.; RILEY, D. W. Using Inventory for Competitive Advantage through Supply Chain Management *. International Journal of Physical Distribution & Materials Management, v. 15, n. 5, p. 16–26, 1985.

LEE, H. A. U. L.; NG, S. H. U. M. Introduction to the special issue on global supply chain management. Production and Operations Managment, v. 6, n. 3, p. 191–192, 1997.

LEE, H. L.; BILLINGTON, C. Managing Supply Chain Inventory Pitfalls and Opportunities. Sloan Management Review, v. 33, n. 3, p. 64–73, 1992.

NEUTZLING, D. M.; NASCIMENTO, L. F. M. DO. Governança em Cadeias de Suprimento Sustentáveis: uma discussão conceitual associada aos aspectos da Coordenação e Colaboração.SIMPOI 2013. Anais...São Paulo: 2013

PADOVANI, C. B. O papel da governaça na cadeia de suprimento automotiva nos formecedores de primeiro e segundo nível. [s.l.] Universidade de São Paulo, 2007.

PILBEAM, C.; ALVAREZ, G.; WILSON, H. The governance of supply networks: a systematic literature review. Supply Chain Management: An International Journal, v. 17, n. 4, p. 358–376, 2012.

RICHEY, R. G. et al. Exploring a Governance Theory of Supply Chain Management: Barriers and Facilitators To Integration. Journal of Business Logistics, v. 31, n. 1, p. 237–256, 10 mar. 2010.

RITTER, T.; GEMÜNDEN, H. G. Interorganizational relationships and networks. Journal of Business Research, v. 56, n. 9, p. 691–697, set. 2003.

RODRIGUES, A. L.; MALO, M. C. Estruturas de Governança e Empreendedorismo Coletivo : o Caso dos Doutores da Alegria. Revista de Administração Contemporânea, v. 10, n. 3, p. 29–50, 2006.

SPINA, G. et al. Past, present and future trends of purchasing and supply management: An extensive literature review. Industrial Marketing Management, v. 42, n. 8, p. 1202–1212, nov. 2013.

TORRES, R. L.; ANTÔNIO, S.; CARIO, F. A governança da cadeia global de valor na indústria automobilística : um estudo de caso. Revista Econômica - Niteroi, v. 14, n. 1, p. 73–91, 2012.

WILLIAMSON, O. E. Transaction-Cost Economics: The Governance of Contractual Relations. Journal of Law and Economics, v. 22, n. 2, p. 233–261, 1979.

WIND, Y.; FUNG, V. K.; FUNG, W. K. Orquestração de redes: criando e gerenciando cadeias de suprimentos globais sem possuí-las. In: O Desafio das Redes Estratégia, Lucro e Risco em Um Mundo Interligado. Porto Alegre: [s.n.]. p. 277–291.

ZHANG, X.; ARAMYAN, L. H. A conceptual framework for supply chain governance. China Agricultural Economic Review, v. 1, n. 2, p. 136–154, 30 jan. 2009.

# Chapter 4.

## Trust and Commitment Basis Relations to the Local Cooperatives

Ernesto M. Giglio,
Nilson Bertoli, Cristiane Veloso,
Eliana C. Tarricone

## Abstract

This research explores the interface between the social categories of trust and commitment, given as the organizing axis of the governance and asymmetry, having the cooperatives of grape and banana production at the north of Paraná State, Brazil, as the objects of study. The work is justified by the theoretical importance of social categories as organizers of small networks configuration, like associations and cooperatives; as well as by the opportunity to examine two networks agribusiness developments in the region. The networked society perspective and the social theory of networks principles were used as theoretical foundations. The methodological argument is the assertion that the network is an adaptive complex system, with some incertitude of its processes and outcomes. The predominantly qualitative and descriptive research was conducted, using interview techniques and secondary data. The results indicated that there is an interface between trust and commitment along with network governance, while the interface with its solutions of asymmetry was not clearly established. The theoretical contribution is to present a model that integrates four categories and is capable to investigate the social relations in cooperatives. The methodological contribution presents the list of indicators on four qualitative categories, which are not founded in academic literature.

## 4.1 Introduction

The aim of this work is to analyze the structural states of networks cooperatives, characterized by its governance and solution of asymmetry, having the social categories of trust and commitment as the axis to organize the network. The field of investigation is the grape and banana cooperatives in the north of Paraná State, Brazil, which is mainly composed by small farmers.

Reviews about networks (Oliver, Ebers, 1998; Giglio; Kwasnicka, 2006; Provan *et al*, 2007) revealed some theories that can be grouped into three main paradigms according to their principles:

(A) Rational and economic, referring to cost factors and resource dependence (Williamson, 1981; Gulati, 1998);

(B) Social and technical, regarding social aspects as basis for decision making (Granovetter, 1985; Uzzi, 1997);

(C) The networked society, stating that business networks are manifestations of a society organized in networks (Nohria, Eccles, 1992; Castells, 2010).

This work uses some complementary statements from the socio-technical approaches and the networked society, considering trust and commitment as important and necessary points to establish networks structures (Larson, 1992; Grandori, Soda, 1995; Gulati, Gargiulo, 1999; Ebers, Jarillo, 1998). The guiding proposition is that the configuration of the network, which is defined by governance and solution of asymmetry, is intrinsically related to the presence of trust and commitment.

The importance of this work is related to the shortage of studies on the social ties involving interface and network structure, especially in the case of small cooperatives. Methodologically, the effort is justified because the systemic perspective is used for network analysis, considering multiple connections and accepting the uncertainties of linear historic development. This perspective is rarely applied in network studies, but is considered appropriate considering the use of social and structural constructs.

## 4.2 Bibliographical review

At the Proquest web portal, a bibliographical research was conducted with the following keywords: 1) Network; 2) Trust; 3) Commitment; 4) Networks States and 5) Agribusiness, Agricultural, Agriculture. The isolated and combined returned matches can be seen in Table 4.1. The conclusion is that works which match the interface between social categories and the selected structures are rare. Considering this result it is undeniable that this work characterizes itself by its uniqueness, which also adds value to it.

Table 4.1. Nominations articles categories in the portal Proquest.

| Categories | Nominations |
|---|---|
| (1) Network | 97,271 |
| (2) Trust | 6851 |
| (3) Commitment | 9,307 |
| (4) Network States | 12,876 |
| (5) Agricultural | 2,373 |
| (1) and (2) | 518 |
| (1) and (3) | 52 |
| (1) and (5) | 50 |
| (2) and (3) | 18 |
| (2) and (4) | 157 |
| (2) and (5) | 0 |
| (3) and (4) | 0 |
| (2) and (4) | 3 |

### 4.2.1 About Trust

Trust category is well investigated in relation networks (Das, Teng, 2004; Beugelsdijk, 2006; Boehe, Balestro, 2006. Giglio et *al,* 2008), being conceptually defined in a range of knowledge including Psychology, in the sense of the psychological disposition to believe in others; the rational and interest definitions, which predict profits when using collective resources; and even social perspectives, which define trust as a relation where one person puts itself in a situation of dependency of another, whether it is for being the weak link, or for the need of the other's resources. This second line of thought will be used in this work. The fact of putting yourself in dependency of another manifests itself in behaviors such as asking for help, exposing one of your company's problems and making resources available to others with no need for any safeguards.

We state that trust is the axis of the network and in which rules are organized, asymmetries are resolved and the efforts are channeled to obtain information as collective results. Commitment is the counterpart of trust.

### 4.2.2 About Commitment

Commitment is investigated with a broad array of conceptual definitions that goes from rational concepts, as to execute what was agreed, including social concepts, as to put the group more important than individual benefits (Lorange, Ross, 1991; Larson, 1992; Mayntz, 1993).The latter definition will be used in this work because it implies the relation between the parts, thus being the contribution from the authors, stating that commitment can be defined as a counterpart of trust (A trusts B, B helps A with no other advantages).

We state that the absence of commitment is the reason for the networks decline and dissolution.

### 4.2.3 About Governance

In network relations, when there is awareness about interdependency and the evidence of conflicts arises by asymmetries, it is necessary to create rules to solve the conflicts, stimulate collective actions and to control opportunistic behaviors. This is how this work conceptualizes the governance. It refers to the rules to stimulate and control the relation between the parties; therefore it is possible research the source of these rules, their specific function of each group, their maintenance and consequences if they were to be broken.

According to Grandori and Soda (1995) governance can be formal and informal. This points out to the formal governance rules that are described in documents, such as contracts and drafts, and it is more frequent in vertical networks, in which companies are in different productive capacity points, with resources and capacities that require some protection. The informal governance indicates the rules that are present in social relations, such as not to betray others trust. Informal governance is more present in horizontal networks of small organizations, in which the leader's behavior (his ethics, for example) becomes an example to be followed, or the fear of an actor to behave opportunistically, to betray the trust of other colleagues.

### 4.2.4 About Solution of conflicts caused by Asymmetry

Organizations are different in many aspects, which characterize the asymmetry in the collective action. The differences can be beneficial when they allow the flow of new ideas, and non-standard solutions that creates interest and innovation in the group. On the other hand, differences can be a problem because they can either determine the participation capacity or not, of some actors.

It is stated that the existence of asymmetry requires parties to seek solutions and create rules in attempt to better organize the group. These solutions can be characterized such as the high level of dominance of some other actors above, or the actions of the exchanging resources to demise asymmetries.

### 4.2.5 About Efforts to investigate Interfaces

After seeking to combine the expressions Trust, Commitment and Network Structure, shown in data presented on Table 1, the amount of hits for each search is around 10,000 for Trust; 8,000 for Commitment; 30,000 for Network and 279 for the combined terms.

These 279 search results were analyzed seeking information through the summary and in the proposals presented in the introduction. The conclusion is that there are few works investigating the interfaces of trust, commitment and network configuration, and there are no models of integration. The works focus on isolated constructs, stating their importance to the development or network results. As evidence in favor of the presented proposal, the social factors of trust and commitment are consistently put as the organizing axis of network structures.

Considering the networks as a complex set of systems, it is less important to isolate one category and more important to search for the categories that act more closely. Following this last perspective we selected four categories and used the expression "network state" as a result of its interaction.

## 4.3 Theoretical review

The review of the terms *social economy, network, trust, commitment, structure, governance, agricultural and agribusiness* when isolated, conducted to thousands of references, while the combination of two words have led to tens; and finally, combining three or four words led to no reference. Thus, we found no single article investigating the four categories, using network theory and researching on the social organizations. The main trend found was about structure, with representations of networks in the social space related to trust and commitment (Lefebvre, 1991; Castells, 2000; Latour, 2005). The articles about governance followed an analogous pattern, but these were less frequent. The few articles we found involving the conjunction of these two trends created what we called *network states*.

### 4.3.1 Theoretical basis for the concept of network state.

The idea of a network state is a dynamic configuration of the network, along with the presence and the content of trust, commitment, governance and asymmetry resolution. It is intended to make the characterization of the network dynamics clear, which does not occur with the use of the word structure, which refers to the design of the network, the defined roles and the position of the actors. Network structure is a subject with numeric variables, such as centrality and density, but does not show any information about the dynamics and the content of relations between actors.

The expression *network states* is rarely used in literature. We found that articles have in common the seeking of variables that would be the network organizers, but every time putting an isolated variable to the base. Given the evidence of the presence of the categories collected from the bibliographical research and the rarity of conjunction models, we proposed the concept of the network state, asset that is characterized by the four categories: trust, commitment, governance and asymmetry; which refer to relationship categories. They are, as stated here, the ones that configure the state or organization of a network, thus being the basis of how the network and the actors decision works.

Reviews on network concepts (Nohria, Eccles, 1992; Jarillo; Ricart, 1988; Miles; Snow, 1992; Oliver; Ebers, 1998; Rusbult, Van Lange, 2003) lead to factors considered essential in the network phenomenon, such as interdependence. This means the need of collective actions, being the trust and commitment categories so important and necessary to network development.

According to Nohria and Eccles (1992) the networks are the current mode to describe and investigate organizations. Granovetter (1985) and Uzzi (1997) assert that technical and commercial actions are inextricably linked to social relations networks. The more the actors are immersed in networks, that is, committed to collective actions and trust relations; the greater the network equilibrium is obtained, once the role definitions and expected behavior were clear.

Those assertive leads to the following principles:

(I) Existence of a new format of society, manifested in networks, having the interdependence as its main fact;

(II) All organizations are in networks, whether their actors develop their connections or not;

(III) Networks are developed on social basis;

(IV) Actors are immersed in networks and they express their level of commitment and trust in the collective objectives, as well as in the behavior with the other actors.

These statements are directed to the relational approach, which is considered capable to investigate small groups, either social or business groups.

## 4.3.2 Trust, commitment, structure and governance interface framework and its operational concepts.

Trust is defined putting oneself in the dependency of another, in its many manifestations, such as asking for help, exposing a problem or a weakness of his organization, and making resources available to others (Morgan, Hunt, 1994).

Commitment is defined as the disposition of a person towards collective actions, without putting its own benefit as the most important and not taking advantage of the trust bestowed (Grandori, Soda, 1995). The choice for this line of definition regarding the relation of trust and commitment is due to colleagues. Both are set as interlaced organized axis, such as DNA chains or the nucleus of an atom, such categories are from where the others further organize.

Governance is a set of rules and incentives created to control people's behaviors and encourage them to remain in the group (Jones *et al.*, 1997).

Solution of asymmetry is defined as the decisions that are made to resolve the conflicts that emerge due to the difference of resource, or objectives between actors.

These categories are consistently defined as the essential in the literature, and they form the nucleus of what characterizes the relationships in the network. Network states will be defined as the combination of these categories in a certain moment of observation, much like a picture. The choice for this expression is regarding to the meaning of the word *state*. It implies to different configurations because in every moment that the network is observed, it can present a picture or a different configuration, depending of the occurred events.

Chart 4.1. shows the model, inspired in the structure of an atom, designed in categories and the axis.

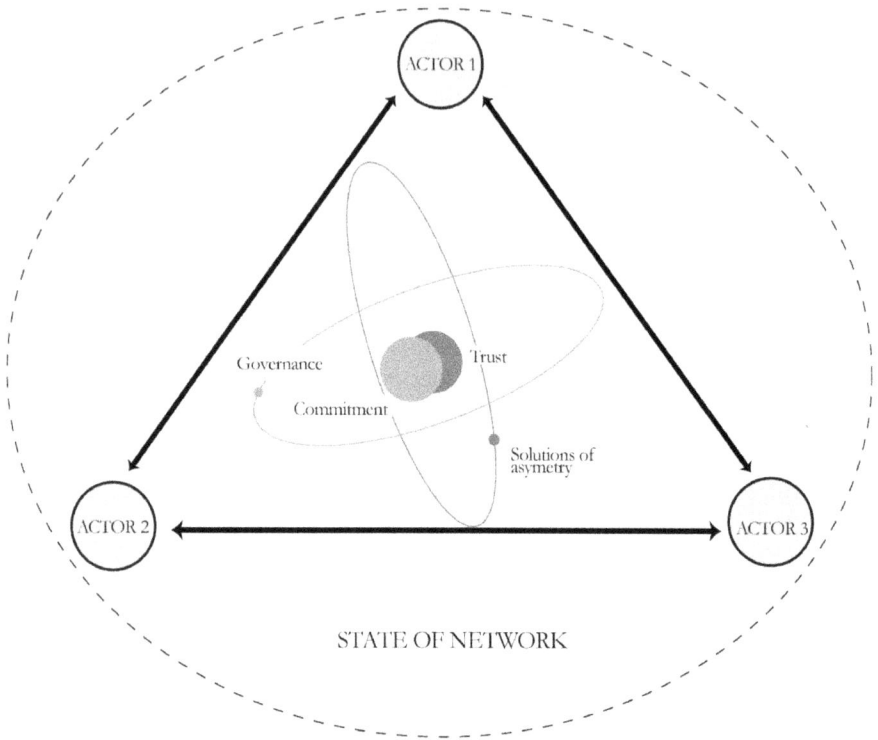

**Chart 4.1 The model of network state configuration, with two axis categories and two complementary categories.**

We also formulated indicators for each category to direct the applied survey. Chat 4.2 presents a list of some indicators used in the interviews.

**Chart 4.2. Categories that define the network state and examples of indicators.**

| Category | Dominant Concept | What is to be Observed | Some Indicators |
|---|---|---|---|
| Commitment | Putting oneself available to collective actions; not taking advantage of others dependencies. | Attitudes and actions to achieve collective goals or to help another player, even with any small profit. | 1. Regular participation on meetings and decisions. 2. Aid the other, even without benefit. 3. Take responsibilities of joint actions. 4. Perception among actors about the fulfillment of agreements. 5. Existence of promises of continuity the relations between partners. 6. Behaviors that show the disposition to the continuity of relationships. |

| | | | |
|---|---|---|---|
| Trust | Putting oneself in dependency of another, or offer his resources to collective use. | Attitudes and actions in which the subject is exposed to the collective; it is dependent on another; or its resources are available without the use of formal control mechanisms. | 1. Weaknesses exposition and dependency toward others. 2. Assumption of responsibility of a task, which execution depends on another, trusting the other will fulfill his part. 3. Make any resources available for collective use, without the need of safeguards. 4. Behaviors to indicate the actor follows the rules and goals established in the network. 5. Behaviors and attitudes to show the actors trust in the integrity of the people who are part of the network. |
| Asymmetries | Differences of capacities and resources, and the solutions to solve the given conflicts. | Differences of any nature which are relevant to the network organization and to resolution ways. | 1. Identification of the most distinct differences between the participants. 2. Difference of invested resources. 3. Difference of objectives. 4. Difference of values and ethics. 5. Difference of technological knowledge. 6. Conflicts and problems that arise due to asymmetries. 7. Ways of conflicts resolution given from asymmetries. |

| Governance | Rules of resource protection and control behavior. It can be formal or informal. | Each and every explicit or implicit rule puts restrictions, or incentive to the behavior, and protects the resources, being either collective or individual. | 1. Rules about admission and exclusion of actors from the most closed group. 2. Rules about penalties. 3. Rules about hierarchy, leadership and operation. 4. Control by authority or reputation (from the most powerful actor, for example). 5. Social controls (such as blogs, community sites and others, with information about the participants). 6. Rules about equality between actors. |

Source: The authors, 2015.

## 4.4 Material and Methods

This research is descriptive and predominantly qualitative. The data was collected from the agribusiness sector, especially at the grapes and banana small businesses in the North of Paraná state, Brazil. We collected secondary data from libraries, syndicates, town hall and offices from the local newspapers and documents. The primary data for its group leaders interviewed support organization technicians, secretaries' township development, and finally, parts of each business group using the Likert-scale type of sentences in the questionnaires. The data was analyzed by content analysis (Bardin, 1993) using thematic analysis technique.

As the first step of this work, a bibliographical research was made on small agribusiness networks. There are many works about agribusiness, agriculture and other similar topics. After a search using the combination of the network expressions, the amount of hits were around 18,000 for Agricultural, 222,000 for Network and 204 for the combined terms.

From these results, it was established the period of search from the last 13 years (2002-2015), which resulted in 132 results that were filtered by subject, which also resulted in 78 close indications. The content of these 78 results was then analyzed and we didn't find any work that investigated the interfaces between the four categories that define the network state. This implies certain uniqueness to the presented work, but also the absence of instruments that could be used as well as results that can be compared.

## 4.5 Results and Discussion

In this section we present relevant information that emerged from analyzing secondary and primary data altogether.

### 4.5.1 Grape cooperative network in Bandeirantes - Paraná state, Brazil

The grape growers from Bandeirantes town have been developed by 105 grape producers. It begun in 1992, with only 12 of them; with a document privileging transparency, in the sense of commitment. This activity gave origin to an association named Adecot, and later Triangle Group emerged from it, which is now the network operational center. Interviews with the local leaders indicated that opportunist behaviors occurred, but they ended up bringing a strong determination for building trust and commitment among actors.

Fifteen interviews were carried out clearly converging towards pointing trust and commitment to the cooperative development base. This result supported the statement about axes. Governance is clearly established and the asymmetry does not cause problems. Interview excerpts illustrate this situation: "... *people trust and learn from each other, when you try to pass news to the other to stay well informed; ... we help everyone if necessary, and whenever the other needs to put a good group of people together to quickly help his friend ; ... the differences you know they are part of our life, difference in thinking, in behavior, but you always have to get a collective solution ... "*

Data was collected from 20 people who answered the questionnaire. The results are organized by the percentage of concordance answers shown in Table 4.2 The high level of the numbers supported the guiding proposition. The numerator expresses the sum of responses "strongly agree" and "agree" and the denominator is the total number of responses.

**Table 4.2: Answers from grape producers showing percentage of concordance about four categories that define the network state.**

|     | Commitment | Trust | Structure | Governance |
| --- | --- | --- | --- | --- |
| **Sum** | 110/140 (78%) | 141/180 (78%) | 52/80 (65%) | 116/180 (64%) |

The interviews made it possible to create a design of the network on social and commercial relations, as shown in Figure 4.3 The central actors, Francisco and Sebastian, are the most often cited as examples of ethics and honesty as well as the most experienced in the business.

**Figure 4.3. The network of social and commercial relations of grape farmers in the state of Parana Brazil**

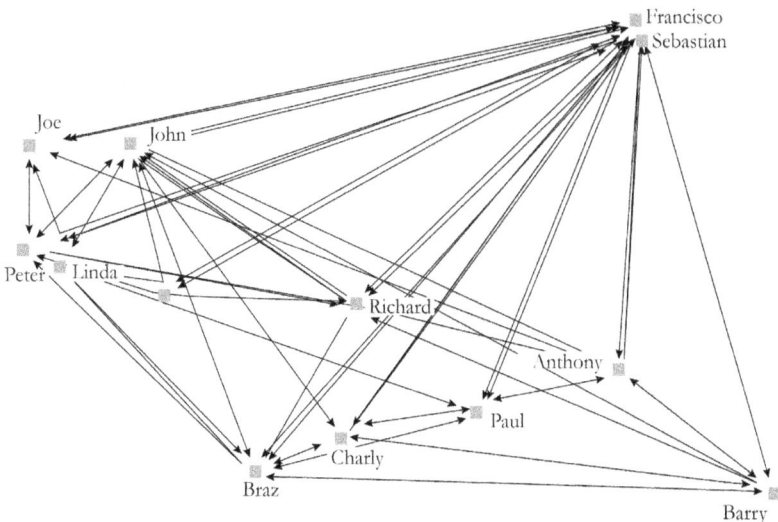

The data was sufficient to sustain the statement that social relations are an important and necessary backdrop for the actions and processes on the network.

### 4.5.2 Banana producers network in Andirá - Paraná State, Brazil

The banana cooperative also initiated in 1992 from an EMATER (Rural Technical Assistance Institute of Paraná) proposal, seeking place for producers in search of new sources of incomes. At the beginning, 50 producers from Andirá town were put together. The group worked informally for 13 years until the foundation of APBANA (Banana producers association of Andirá and Region) in 2008. The group has currently 16 members. Interviews with the local leaders indicated that the business was powered by the local government actions more than by the producers' initiative. We analyzed that this fact is one of the reasons why the group has only grown some years after the first harvest results.

Eleven interviews were carried out and showed some confluence in trust and commitment to the cooperative development base. Governance is not clearly established once there is presence of some opportunistic behavior, and the asymmetry does not cause problems. Here is an interview excerpt that illustrates this situation: *"we are held together, and trust each other, everyone is a friend ... we already had too much trouble to run after all, and the guy was there and just took profit, we are trying to solve and converse; we were trying not to disaggregate... will find only problem the guy who is not engaged and does not seek the help of the group, if you want to work isolated ... there will always be differences in the group, each one is each one, they cannot just let it increase and harm the group"*

Differently from the grape growers, in this group soon emerged the figure of the intermediary (broker) that is also a producer and profits from both sources. Data from 10 people who answered the questionnaire are displayed in Table 4.3 following the same structure of Table 4.2.

**Table 4.3: Answers from banana producers showing percentage of concordance about four categories that define the network state.**

|  | Commitment | Trust | Structure | Governance |
|---|---|---|---|---|
| Sum | 56/70 (80%) | 75/90 (83%) | 20/40 (50%) | 64/90 (71%) |

The interviews made possible to create a design of the network of social and commercial relationships for this banana group, as shown in Figure 4. The central actors are seen as the most experienced and those that serve as examples of honesty and integrity.

**Figure 4.4. The network of social and commercial relations of the banana farmers in the state of Parana Brazil**

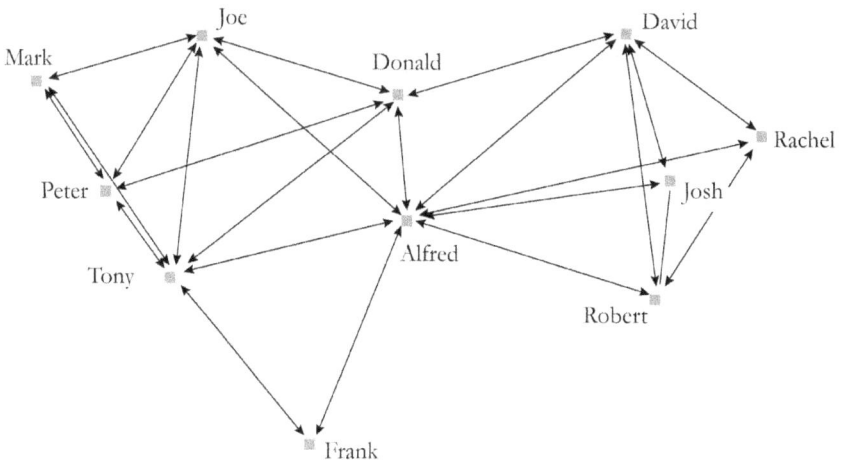

Considering the data gathered at both settings, we can assert that the guiding proposition was more supported by the network grape cooperative than the banana cooperative. Nevertheless, the following conclusions refer to the grape as well as to the banana cooperative network.

(A) Data sustained the guiding proposition on the presence of trust, commitment, governance and solution of asymmetry categories at both small networks.

(B) Percentages above 60% at all categories are clearly set for the grape producers' network, while for the banana network the solution relation of asymmetry was not clearly determined.

(C) Using the theoretical basis statements, we concluded affirmatively that both small networks cooperatives have a distinct development pathway, culminating in two different states of networks. There is more participation in group meetings, as well as more information exchange and mutual help among actors in the grape producer's network than there is in the banana network. These results lead to higher levels, formal and informal organization involving governance, and providing a higher equilibrium among the grape producers network. Also, the existence of an internal subgroup with decision power is a characteristic of the grape producer network. In the banana network, there is less participation in meetings from the actors, and weaker signals of mutual help and information exchange. In addition, we could notice indications of dominance of a competition culture, considering the intermediary presences among producers, competing for the same network profits.

(D) Indicators proposed and the related data collection instruments demonstrated applicability and validity. Still, the data analysis showed that the questionnaire could be improved to become a valid instrument investigation of the proposed interfaces.

## 4.6 Conclusion

The work achieved its objective in answering topics about the conjunction between the social relations of trust and commitment, and the presence of governance and the solution asymmetry categories of small network, being the ways to organize businesses. Data was collected from two family cooperatives in the Northern region of Paraná State, with grape and banana producers.

The statement about the presenting distinct states of network organization was proved. The grape business has a long history between social involvement of participants, either of complete trust (such as offer the entire production without setting prices in anticipation), or opportunism (such as establishing secondary business without letting the group know). These events resulted in a strong cohesion among actors and equally strong social control. By contrast, the banana business has the history of the local governmental entities participation and, as a consequence, collective goals have hardly existed; thus cohesion among participants was weaker.

The theoretical framework was founded in the networked society (Castells, 2010; Nohria, Eccles, 1992) and in the social paradigm of networks (Granovetter 1985; Grandori, Soda, 1995). It was considered able to explain the distinct organizations from both groups, besides giving support to the research instrument construction. Applying these premises about small network existence, we can affirm that the state of grape producer's network presents certain stability and equilibrium, with defined structure, governance, solutions of asymmetry and flows that balance technical, commercial, and social contents. By contrast, the banana producers' network state is characterized by lesser balance and stability.

The theoretical contribution of this work is to indicate interfaces between categories that are normally investigated separately. Even though Granovetter (1985) and Nohria and Eccles (1992) have affirmed that all organizations are in networks, that there is always a social background for any technical behavior; the findings of this work have made little advance in this matter. One of the possible reasons is the difficulty to find valid and applicable instruments. In this sense, the methodological contribution offered by this work is the use of a questionnaire generated from indicators, able to distinguish the state of both networks studied. Previously it has been declared that the operationalization of these categories was not found in academic literature. Nevertheless, the fact that there was theoretical and methodological advances demands the continuity of research to improve the proposed contributions.

# References

BARDIN, L. 1993. L'analyse de contenu. Paris: Presses Universitaires.

BEUGELSDIJK, S. 2006. A note on the theory and measurement of trust in explaining differences in economic growth. Cambridge Journal of Economics, 30: 371–387.

BOEHE, D.; BALESTRO, M. 2006. A dimensão nacional dos custos de transação: oportunismo e confiança institucional. REAd, 49, 12: 1-20.

CASTELLS, M. 2010. The rise of the network society. United Kingdom: Wiley-Blacwell.

_____. 2000. Materials for an exploratory theory of the network society. British Journal of Sociology, 51, 1: 5-24.

DAS, T.; TENG, B. 2004. The risk-based view of trust: a conceptual framework. Journal of Business and Psychology, 19, 1:85-116.

EBERS, M., JARILLO, J. C. 1998. The construction, forms, and consequences of industry networks. International Studies of Management and Organization, 27, 4: 3-21.

GIGLIO, E.; KWASNICKA, E. 2006. Proposta de integração do consumidor na teoria e prática de redes. Anais do XXX EnANPAD.

GIGLIO, E. et al. 2008. Reflexões sobre os fatores relevantes no nascimento e no crescimento de redes de negócios na agropecuária. Organizações Rurais & Agroindustriais, 10, 2: 279-292.

GRANDORI, R., SODA, G. 1995. Interfirms networks: antecedents, mechanisms, and forms. Organization Studies, 16, 2: 183-214.

GRANOVETTER, M. 1985. Economic Action and Social Structure: The Problem of Embeddedness. The American Journal of Sociology, 91, 3: 481-510.

GULATI, R. 1998. Alliances and networks. Strategic Management Journal, 19, 4: 293-317.

GULATI, R., GARGIULO, M. 1999. Where Do Interorganizational Networks Come From? The American Journal of Sociology, 104, 5: 1439-1493.

JARILLO, J., RICART, J. 1988. On Strategic Networks. Strategic Management Journal, 9, 1: 31-41.

JONES, C., HESTERLY, W., BORGATTI, S. 1997. A general theory of network governance: Exchange conditions and social mechanisms. Academy of Management Review, 22, 4: 911-945.

LARSON, A. 1992. Network dyads in entrepreneurial settings: A study of the governance of exchange relationships. Administrative Science Quarterly, 37, 1: 76-104.

LATOUR, B. 2005. Reassembling the social. Oxford: Oxford Press.

LEFEBVRE, H. 1991. The production of space. Oxford: Blackwell.

LORANGE, P.; ROOS, J. 1991. Analytical steps in the formation of strategic alliances. Journal of Organizational Change Management, 4, 1:60-72.

MAYNTZ, R. 1993. Modernization and the logic of interorganizational networks. Knowledge and Policy, 6, 1:3-16.

MILES, R., SNOW, C. 1992. Causes for Failure in Network Organizations. California Management Review, 34, 1: 53-57.

MORGAN, R., HUNT, S. 1994. The commitment-trust theory of relationship marketing. The Journal of Marketing, 58: 20-38.

NOHRIA, N.; ECCLES, R. 1992. Networks and Organizations: structure, form and action. Boston: Harvard Business School Press.

OLIVER, A.; EBERS, M. 1998. Networking network studies: an analysis of conceptual configurations in the study of inter-organizational relationships. Organization Studies, 19, 4: 549-583.

PROVAN, K., FISH, A., SYDOW, J. 2007. Interorganizational networks at the network level: A review of the empirical literature on whole networks. Journal of Management, 33, 3: 479-516.

RUSBULT, C., VAN LANGE, P. 2003. Interdependence, interaction, and relationships. Annual Review of Psychology, 54, 1: 351-375.

UZZI, B. 1997. Social structure and competition in interfirm networks: The paradox of embeddedness. Administrative Science Quarterly, 42, 1: 35-67.

WILLIAMSON, O. 1981. The economics of organization: the transaction cost approach. American Journal of Sociology, 87, 3: 548-577.

# Chapter 5.

## Contributions from Social Network Approach and Relationship Marketing to Improve Market Results

Celso A. Rimoli,
Thais C. Ravasi,
Claudia Rosa M. Velozo,
Felipe M. G. Freitas.

### Resume

This paper aims at identifying the network approach and relationship marketing contributions to achieve better market results. The network elements analyzed were: intensity of relations, reciprocity, multiplexity and clarity of expectations. As for relationship marketing, we used the KMV Model (Morgan and Hunt 1994). According to the model, the relationship between organizations should be mediated by trust and commitment, which allow the antecedent variables (relationship termination costs, relationship benefits, shared values, communication and opportunistic behavior) effectively reach the consequent ones (increase in acquiescence , cooperation and functional conflict, and decrease in propensity to leave and uncertainty). The research was exploratory and qualitative with a single-case study of the trajectory of Porto Ferreira Ceramics. Based on the results it was possible to show that the combination of network elements and relationship marketing, especially trust and commitment are present in a subtle, but essential way to obtain the best results of marketing actions.

### 5.1 Introduction

Competing in block, which means operating as a network in a context marked by frequent and important changes - technological, social and economic - means to have greater access to resources and information than doing it alone would allow . Joint action through partnerships, alliances or strategic network leads to levels of competitiveness that are hard to be achieved as an isolated player because of gains obtained from cooperation and interdependence (Nohria, Ecles, 1992; Morgan, Hunt, 1994; Ebers; Jarillo, 1998; Gulati;

Gargiulo, 1999). When acting in networks, companies learn to share power, striving to use their position in the network to win access to information and resources that are useful to all (Nohria, Ecles, 1992).

The connections formed by social relations between actors were already studied in business networks well before the competitive theories of the 1980s (Tichy; Tushman; Fombrun, 1979). These ideas gained strength and visibility to the current situation, marked by several changes of various types, favoring the emergence of networks. Those changes contributed to the formation of a social structure based on connections, the networked society (Castells, 2000). They impacted, among other business processes, the marketing activities of companies belonging to various industries, including ceramics. Apparently the competition in this industry is in an isolated basis, but there is evidence that relationships between suppliers, buyers, sellers, etc., have a prominent role in it. Therefore, this chapter examines these aspects in the case of the company Cerâmica Porto Ferreira Ceramics in order to achieve the following general objective: to identify the network approach and relationship marketing contributions to achieve better market results. The specific objectives are: a) Relating similarities, complementarities and differences between the network approach and relationship marketing; b) Identifying elements and network variables in the relationships between the actors; and c) Identifying how the elements and variables of networks and relationship marketing contribute to the effectiveness of marketing activities.

## 5.2 Theoretical framework

The conceptual basis of the chapter has elements of the social network approach, relationship marketing and metrics to measure results.

### 5.2.1. Networks

Networking is a quite common term today due to the popularity of social networking sites like *Facebook* and *Twitter,* but this concept has been used in various fields of knowledge (anthropology, psychology, sociology, health, etc.) since the 1930s. Despite the popularity of social networks like

Facebook and Twitter, in this chapter a network is understood as a system of objects or actors made up of people, groups or organizations together by various relationships. Not all actors are interlinked and some have multiple relationships (Tichy, Tushman and Fombrun 1979). Social influence may be reciprocal, including elements of leadership and authority among companies, as well as interpersonal relationships (Grandori; Soda, 1995).

Due to the aspects to be examined in this chapter, the social approach was adopted, which is focused on social relationships established among actors, based on factors such as trust and commitment. A closer linkage, made of strong ties, as Granovetter (1983) called, brings benefits to the network regarding the great level of trust and commitment among actors, but there is a possibility that implies lack of openness to new ideas. Following there are some structural elements of networks (Tichy, Tushman and Fombrun 1979) which are important for the analytical part of the chapter.

Transactional content. It represents what is exchanged among social actors, and could be affection (love, friendship), influence or power, information, or goods and services

Nature of the links. It refers to the strength of the relationship between social actors and it is described by the following characteristics: intensity, reciprocity or degree of symmetry; clarity of expectations, multiplexity or assuming multiple roles in the network.

Structural characteristics. They serve as a reference for the relations between the actors. They are of four types: internal network, external network, *cluster* within the network (working groups, emerging coalitions and 'cliques') and individuals that act as key people in the network.

### 5.2.2 Relationship Marketing

Relationship marketing emphasizes collaboration between partners in the competition process (Parvatiyar; Sheth, 2000), which also occurs in the networking approach, as seen. This collaboration is key to the success of the actions planned in several markets such as industrial in which relationships permeate much of the marketing process (Harker and Egan, 2006).

According to Grönroos (2006), for years the marketing literature has been divided between the transactional paradigm, once-dominant and the relational, whose studies grew. The author suggests that companies should understand the dynamics of their markets and, depending on the situation, use the resources of transactional or relational paradigm. Harker and Egan (2006) and Gummesson (2005) also suggest this hybrid approach because they are not mutually exclusive, but complementary. Thus, understanding relationship marketing as business philosophy means engaging collective efforts so that all people involved achieve their individual and collective goals, based on effective relationships (Silva et al., 2012).

Regarding companies, the boundary between social and professional relationships is partially erased. The friendship is between people who talk to each other, and also help and trust each other spending a good time together. This also occurs in commercial relationships in which components of trust can be developed (Gummesson, 2005).

### 5.2.3. Networking and relationship marketing approach : complementarities

The principles underlying the network approach and relationship marketing have similarities and complementarities, so that it is possible to establish connections between them. For example, it was seen that for Castells (2000), changes in society have led individuals and companies to establish new liaisons that resulted in interconnections among the actors, denominated network society. Similarly, Gummesson (2005) classifies the interaction and relationships between actors as the basis for a more effective form of marketing practice, as he also sees society as a network of relationships. And both believe there must be cooperation among the actors for this to occur.

As a complement, Morgan and Hunt (1994) argue that the success of a network is the result of cooperative efforts built on the commitment and trust between actors. Commitment results from trust established among actors, and leads to cooperation through social relationships. If the relationship is deemed important to them, everything possible to keep it will be done. Granovetter (1985) pitch in to this notion placing that the commitment among the actors of a network appears informally in social relations, is maintained by ties such as friendship and is sustained on trust, which leads to cooperation.

According to Palmatier et al. (2009), the proximity between the parties involved in an agreement, work, sales or communication helps to build trust, and the relationships based in it are superior to others because the level of satisfaction with the relationship is greater. Perry (2005) also states that one way to get good results in business is mutual cooperation, based on trust and commitment. This is similar to the principles of network theory, as it has been explained before in this chapter, and it shows that relationships can improve the company's marketing results. Thus network theory resembles relationship marketing because relationships provides the exchange of resources between the actors that form the network.

### 5.2.3.1 Model KMV: Key Mediating Variables

The key point of Morgan and Hunt Ideas (1994) lies on the fact that to occur exchanges, the relationship must be based on trust and commitment, understood as mediating variables that allow the backgrounds (on the left in Figure 5.1) can be led to the consequents, or results (on the right in Figure 5.1).This is the essence of KMV Model (Key Mediating Variables)

**Figure 5.1. The KMV Model**

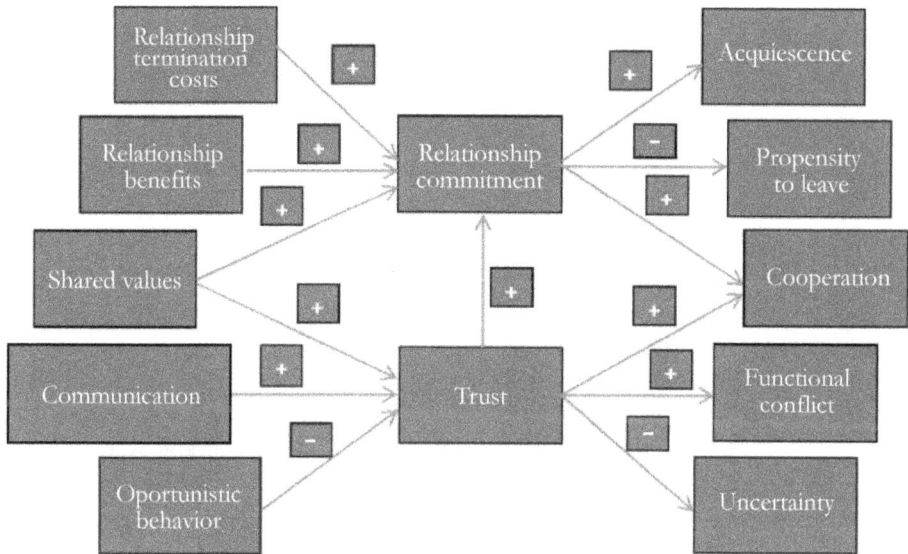

**Source: Morgan and Hunt, 1994.**

The model shows that if the partners possessed similar values, communication were healthy and there were no opportunism, then there are good conditions for trust to occur. In addition, commitment does not come only from trust and its antecedents, but also from the effects of the values and beliefs of shared partners.

Regarding cooperation, more than half of the differences in the levels of this variable would be explained by the commitment and trust relations and their antecedents. Morgan and Hunt (1994) state that even knowing the partners, sharing values and existing trust and commitment, there is no success guarantee for relationship marketing in the global economy. However, it is certain that in the age of networked competition, being alone and opting for short term gains and opportunism lead to failure.

In short, success in relationship marketing involves cooperation, which is based on trust and commitment. And because of that the KMV model was chosen for the analysis of this study.

### 5.2.4 Marketing metrics

Ambler and Kokkinaki (1997) identified several metrics to measure marketing results, the main ones being: sales, market share, profit, preferred brand and purchase intent. The authors recommend considering the following attributes in the choice of metrics: the type of business, the type of customers involved and the planning style. Farris et al. (2007) subsequently created a set of metrics grouped into nine categories, from consumer and market perceptions, including management of the marketing mix to the financial analysis of the marketing programs.

The metrics model used in this chapter is based on Ambler and Kokkinaki (1997) ideas, and involves the knowledge of the company's business and the customer, the percentage of sales and market share. This was due to the fact that the researched company practices such indicators, and has consolidated available information for this study.

### 5.3 Methodological Approach

This study is qualitative and exploratory. The research strategy adopted was case study research, for understanding the dynamics presented in a single setting (Eisenhardt, 1989), and it is indicated when there is a current context of study, it is not possible to have full control over the variables and the research question is' how 'or why' (Yin, 2010).

Following the procedures of the method, the case study protocol was built up with all its constituent elements. As recommended by Yin (2010) and Martins and Theóphilo (2009), data collection had various sources of evidence, specifically: document analysis, personal interviews and participant observation. Interviewed actors were the company's marketing manager, a sales representative, sales promoters, retailers and a representative of the National Association of Construction Material Traders (Anamaco). Next the follow-up meetings in the Retail School Anamaco (SP) were observed which brought sales promoters, sales representatives, supervisors and managers. In addition to observing the posture and the relationship of these actors, it was possible to talk to promoters, sales representatives and the person that represented Anamaco. The data analysis conducted was pattern matching technique (Yin, 2010), being defined as the basis to compare and analyze the conceptual content of the chapter, which describes concepts of networks, relationship marketing and some marketing metrics.

## 5. 4. Presentation of the collected data

Secondary information are Initially presented, followed by the results of interviews with the marketing manager, four sale promoters, a sales representative, a retailer and a representative of Anamaco, and finally the findings of participant observation.

### 5.4.1 Secondary information about the white ceramic industry and the company

Porto Ferreira Ceramics, based in Porto Ferreira city, São Paulo State, Brazil, has great prominence on the national scene in this industry and concentrates its production away from regions that manufacture ceramic tiles: Criciuma (SC) and Mogi Guaçu and Santa Gertrudes (SP). Traditionally these companies compete on the basis of technology, leaving a gap in relationships (ANFACER, 2011). Founded in 1931, the company has held the first market position in sales for a long time, then it went into a crisis and bankrupted twice. Its recovery from the 13th to the 5th position in its market was due to trust in its brand and the relationships established when the marketing department was formally created.

The recovery occurred with the substitution of the Superintendence and the Commercial Director and also assistance of a consulting company, when

Porto Ferreira was facing its second bankruptcy. Career plans were designed to value employees who were not properly recognized until then. Another important action was to restructure the sales force, hiring and training new promoters and creating promotional material to improve the relationship of Porto Ferreira Ceramics with its major customers and the building material stores.

Aiming to reach the goals proposed in the marketing plan, the Blue Wave Project was created, involving all areas of the company. It was started in the National Sales Convention, which was attended by almost all people involved, internal and external employees, sales representatives and sales promoters. As a result, there was an approximation of the company's areas and the confidence instilled in all participants, as they became active participants in the upcoming changes.

Thus, the project reinforced the principles disclosed by Morgan and Hunt (1994) that the success of each partner brings to the success of the network. Therefore, the management of relationships with those involved in the project was essential. Later the Blue Wave project was expanded to other areas of the company resulting in less waste, streamlined processes, reduction of non-compliance of products and improved relationship between retailers, vendors and consumers. These actions have increased trust in the company and generated commitment among stakeholders leading to success.

It also important to highlight the creation of Retail University of Porto Ferreira Ceramics, unprecedented project in the segment designated to provide continuing training to employees and their direct customers. The company values its human capital and it needed to adapt it to new opportunities, moving the market also via education. A training notebook was created with important business information in didactic format and organized courses on the skills that needed to be developed.

## 5.4.2 Primary information: interviews reporting relationships status

According to the marketing manager, although there is a customer service channel to ask questions or make complaints, it is still of little use by consumers. Therefore when there are requests or inquiries, they are always readily met. The company has good relationships with shopkeepers who are driven by sales managers together with representatives and they are all considered as partners. The shopkeepers recognize the reputation of the company as a supplier and the result can be measured by the volume of sales orders. About the influence of sales representatives over their peers, the shopkeepers said they have little contact to each other, which takes place once a year at the Fair Revestir. It was reported that in this group (about 80 people in the country), some stand out more than others. The marketing manager said that the representatives have good relationships with retailers (building supply stores), because they consider them as partners. For him Anfacer hardly influences the marketing activities, because it focuses on industry and not in retail. To him Anamaco influences when it publishes information about the company or its products in the association magazine.

Regarding the sales promoters, there is a healthy competition, which encourages them all to reach the goals and not to disputes where only one wins. The answer to what influences more the attainment of goals varied from salary to challenge. Promoter B which was driven by challenges, emphasized that her supervisor has an important role in the process because she relies on the work of the promoters and always say, "Look, I trust you, ok?!". Asked if that motivated her, the response was enthusiastic: "Wow, and how!." All interviewed believed that they exert influence on marketing decisions as important part of the company. All interviewed people showed that the relationship among them and that they are also partners of the company. When asked if they consider themselves committed to the company, as all answered yes, although promoter D declared she was not entirely in accordance with the prices of some products but she has always tried to convince consumers, proving her commitment.

The sales representative interviewed is at the company for 13 years, she started as a sales promoter, and her team consists of nine sales promoters. The relationship between them is friendly, sometimes even funny, as she had been a sales promoter, and knows the difficulties and the wrong things. She has always sought to have good relationships with vendors, developers and shop owners, so that the results are satisfactory. The relationship between the representatives is a great exchange of information and dialogue on issues and material support. About who influences more the success of a marketing action she said it was teamwork. The representative made clear the commitment of all parties involved, aiming at good results.

The interviewed shopkeeper said his relationship with the company was excellent, both in the company-customer communication, as in a personal sense. And he enthuses to say that he was asked by the company about the difficulties and what customers want as new products and stresses that "It is the first time I've seen this happening in 28 store years."

Finally, the representative of Anamaco, responsible for the Retail School space, where the Porto Ferreira holds monthly meetings with the sales promoters and representatives pointed out that the relationship - described as a partnership - with the company is "very good".

### 5.4.3 Participant observation

This data collection technique showed that the profile of groups varies from retail to retail. Ages also vary, ranging from just over 20 years to about 60, with a predominance of women in their 40s. Almost all the time, the promoters remained attentive while representatives spoke. We noticed significant interaction between them, one of the elements that led to acting in networks and relationship marketing.

## 5.5 Data analysis

This section provides analysis and commentary on the material collected in the field based on the concepts that explain the relationship between network approach and relationship marketing, as indicated in item 5.3, Methodological approach.

### 5.5.1 Network Elements

According to the fundamental properties proposed by Tichy, Tushman and Fombrun (1979), the transactional content between the actors described in the case of Porto Ferreira Ceramics can be understood as information and influences. The main actors are the marketing manager, the communications manager with the market and sales managers, influencing each other and also the sales promoters, sales supervisors and representatives, who receive, disclose and put information to practice.

Analyzing the nature of the links, there had been intensity of relationship for all surveyed actors, they were committed to the obligations, that is, to fulfill in the responsibilities. Reciprocity could be seen in the marketing manager's relationship with the promoters and vice versa. The manager heard what promoters had to say because they were in direct contact with the end consumer; promoters, meanwhile, were aware of this responsibility and suggested what they thought it was important for management and influence the buying decision of consumers. Another relationship in which reciprocity is explicitly shown is between promoters and representatives. Each party needed the other to perform a well-done job, so there's reciprocal influence among them. The same type of reciprocity was true for the sales promoters and the shopkeeper. Reciprocity to the company was lesser only with Anamaco, represented by the marketing manager, because he does not believe that it influences the success of marketing actions of the company; however, Anamaco believed this influence exists. Nevertheless, for everyone to be successful, everyone has a role and seeks to p erform it in the best way.

Regarding the <u>clarity of expectations,</u> each part was aware of what the other expected, which was confirmed by all actors. This feature was pointed out strongly in respect of sales, marketing and communication managers with the market, but less intensity regarding the relationship between marketing manager and Anamaco, for example.

The <u>multiplexity</u> variable appears in the relationship among some actors, such as the sales representatives and sales promoters. The former take on the roles of representing the brand at the point of sale (POS), negotiating with the shopkeeper and managing the team of promoters who operates in the POS that he visits. The marketing manager has multiple roles: when in contact with Anamaco, he represents the company and not just the marketing department. The retailer, who only assumed the role of having the product available to the final consumer, recently assumed the role of participanting in the creation of new products, as the interviewed retailer mentioned: "It is the first time I've seen this happening in 28 years in the shop ... hearing the opinion of the retailer to create a new product that the market is in need."

### 5.5.2 Relationship marketing variables according to the KMV Model

This part of the analysis is divided into antecedent and consequent variables of the KMV Model (Morgan et Hunt, 1994). Following, the antecedent variables are analyzed.

**Relationship termination costs:** it is positive to the relationship and it is identified when the manager states that the price is given by the market and that they seek to adequate their products to what it is practiced in this market. When planning sales, there is also the participation of the entire sales team.

**Relationship benefits:** They are perceived positively by the importance of the participation of salespeople, sales promoters and supervisors so that the goals are met. The first point is how the current manager perceives its employees: as associates, not as employees. It is not just speech, the values shared between manager and marketing director, sales managers, sales representatives and promoters are identified by the team unity and reinforce their commitment.

**Shared values:** They relate to the culture of the organization, which evolves and adapts. Thus, in the previous administration, one of the main values was the resources being directed to production, but always acting ethically and honestly, thus offering quality products. In relation to the current administration, the difference lies in the fact that the manager appreciates people and understands they are a fundamental part of the company processes

**Communication:** This is also positive. It involves planning and aims to cover the entire company. This is what is identified at the monthly meetings with the promoters and the sales team as well as the visits that sales managers do to resellers throughout Brazil. Information should circulate and be confirmed to carry no mistakes.

**Opportunistic behavior:** This item appears as negative due to the fact that its absence favors the overall result of the antecedent variables. According to the marketing manager, he has always been receptive to competitors. He said that once one of them came to visit the company to see how the University of Retail was created. All information was given, but it has not yet been put into practice because the procedure is quite laborious.

The antecedent variables analyzed showed consistency to the KMV Model and this indicates that the relationship goes to the acquiescence and cooperation, two of the consequent variables. As can be noted in the following analysis of these variables, uncertainty, conflict and propensity to leave can be identified, but to a small degree.

**Propensity to leave:** The propensity to leave appears negatively, which is positive to the relationship. The sharing of values among the network actors favors commitment through trust, leading the relationship to cooperation.

**Functional conflict:** The dispute between the parties can compromise the results of exchanges in the relationship. Within Porto Ferreira Ceramics, this conflict was perceived mildly at the testimony of two promoters interviewed. Promoter A cited the little dispute regarding bonuses; and promoter D mentioned that Porto Ferreira products were very expensive and that she believed that the monthly meetings are tiring and did not bring results that offset. Among the rest involved, this was not perceived.

**Uncertainty:** It is reduced by trust and it was perceived that trust exists between promoters and other actors, such as the sales supervisor, the sales representative and the communication and marketing managers. This is because the promoters feel free to suggest and give opinions to the others on the company's products and marketing, which was confirmed by the sales representatives interviewed.

**Acquiescence:** It is perceived through the existing trust in relationships among actors. As examples it could be mentioned the positive reaction of promoters, retailers and shopkeepers when the Blue Wave was launched and, more recently, with the presentation of the new HD line for promoters.

**Cooperation:** It is fundamental for the results to appear and for the relationships to continue. Therefore, the choice of partners, as in the case of promoters, retailers and shopkeepers, is a critical and fundamental element for success. Moreover, by declaring values such as the importance that employees have to the current manager, working with clarity and transparency, the result is that cooperation is favored.

### 5.5.3 Complementarities and discrepancies between relationship marketing and networks for the best results of marketing actions

From the case studied it is possible to see that variables such as trust, commitment and cooperation are points of intersection between the network approach and relationship marketing. Both have the same function, which is to sustain relationships and maintain partnerships. Thus the intensity of the relationship may be compared to commitment itself, because the higher the first is, the higher the second as well. Reciprocity appears as the following variables: benefits of relationship, communication and shared values, for if two or more actors know what to expect from each other and the values they represent, there are more chances to influence and be influenced according to these values. If clarity of expectations is not well identified and worked in the group, it can lead to opportunistic behavior by increasing the propensity to leave. And the multiplexity variable, representing the various roles that the same actor can play in the process, could be more present as an element in relationship marketing. By the network theory, a network never ends and the principle of the KMV Model is to allow relationships to always be renewed.

### 5.5.4 Results

Following are the main results that the company obtained with the actions developed from the concepts of networking and relationship marketing between 2007 and 2011.

<u>Blue Wave project:</u> In the recovery from the crisis, it generated a 35% increase in the portfolio of active clients, which seems to be linked to: a) perception of higher value of the product in the consumer's vision, which improved average sales price and the retailer margin; b) optimization of the display area at the POS, enabling the conquest of new areas of product display in the main retailers segment; c) an increase of 48.3% in gross sales; d) increase of 33.3% in sales per square meter.

<u>University of Retail:</u> It united suppliers, agents, promoters and retailers, leading to 90% increase in sales and 120% of the customer base one year after its creation.

### 5.6 Conclusion

The study investigated how the contributions of the network approach and relationship marketing can improve the results of marketing actions from the perspective of the network society. Similarities and convergences were found between network approach and relationship marketing in the conceptual part. Among them, there are the proximity that favors partnerships and joint action through strategic alliances or networks to increase quality, efficiency and effectiveness, which is more difficult competing alone (Morgan, Hunt, 1994). In addition, actors get together to ensure the exchange of resources between them and the rest of the market, which involves the company, suppliers, brokers, support institutions, etc. In network theory and relationship marketing cooperation is fundamental, and it comes from trust and commitment, which are basic factors also in the KMV Model. Thus, the success of a network of relationships is the result of cooperative efforts erected on these two main bases (Tichy, Tushman and Fombrun 1979; Morgan and Hunt, 1994; Gummesson; 2005).

In the data analysis collected from the actors, all the chosen network elements have been identified, where the intensity of the relationship and the clarity of expectations showed great convergence, indicating high degree of commitment by the actors. There were few contrary results, such as reciprocity, which appeared as a disadvantage to only one of the actors; and multiplexity, which appears negative for three actors. But these elements are not crucial in the relationship because the multiple roles were not decisive for the results.

The application of the KMV Model allowed showing the relationship between networks and relationship marketing in the market actions of Porto Ferreira Ceramics, which are based on trust and commitment, common to both approaches and leading to cooperation. Thus, it is understood that the actors wanted to build cooperative relationships with its business partners trusting and committing to each other, which led this to better marketing results

We consider that the objectives of this research have been achieved, but the results are valid only within the studied company and not for the industry as a whole, due to the fact that this is a single case study. However, it is possible to replicate the research in future work, which can confirm and extend the knowledge so far.

# References

AMBLER, T.; KOKKINAKI, F. Measures of marketing success. Journal of Marketing Management, v.13, 1997.

ASSOCIAÇÃO BRASILEIRA DE CERÂMICA. Acesso em 25 mar. 2012. http://www.abceram.org.br/site/index.php?area=2&submenu=19

ASSOCIAÇÃO NACIONAL DOS COMERCIANTES DE MATERIAL DE CONSTRUÇÃO - ANAMACO. www.anamaco.com.br. Acesso em: 20 fev. 2011.

ASSOCIAÇÃO NACIONAL DOS FABRICANTES DE CERÂMICA PARA REVESTIMENTOS – ANFACER. www.anfacer.com.br. Acesso em 19 fev. 2011.

BANCO NACIONAL DO DESENVOLVIMENTO - BNDES. Panorama do Setor de Revestimentos Cerâmicos. Set. 2006. Disponível em: www.bndes. gov.br/SiteBNDES/export/.../rs_rev_ceramicos.pdf. Acesso em 20 fev. 2011.

CASTELLS, M. Materials for an exploratory theory of the network society. British Journal of Sociology, v. 51, n. 1, 2000, p. 5–24.

EBERS, M.; JARILLO, J. C. The construction, forms and consequents of industry network. International Studies of Management & Organizations, v.27, n.4, winter, p.3-21, 1997-98

EISENHARDT, K. M. Building theories from case study research. The Academy of Management Review, v. 14, n. 4, p. 532-550, oct.1989.

FARRIS, P. W.; BENDLE, N.T.; PFEIFER, P.E.; REIBSTEIN, D.J. Métricas de marketing: mais de 50 métricas que todo executivo deve dominar. Porto Alegre: Bookman, 2007.

GRANDORI, A; SODA, G. Inter-firm networks: Antecedents, mechanisms and forms. Organization Studies, v.16, n.2, p.183-214, 1995.

GRANOVETTER, M. The Strength of weak ties: a network theory revisited, Sociological Theory, v. 1, 1983, 201-233.

_____. M. Economic action and social structure: The problem of embeddedness. The American Journal of Sociology, v.91, n.3, Nov., p. 481-510, 1985.

GRONROOS, C. On defining marketing: finding a new roadmap for marketing. Marketing Theory, v. 6, n. 4, p. 395-417, 2006.

GULATI, R.; GARGIULO, M. Where do interorganizational networks come from? The American Journal of Sociology, v.104, n.5, Mar., p.1439-1493, 1999.

GUMMESSON E. Marketing de relacionamento total: gerenciamento de marketing, estratégias de relacionamento e abordagem de CRM para a economia de rede. 2 ed. Porto Alegre: Bookman, 2005.

HARKER, M.J.; EGAN, J. The Past, Present and Future of Relationship Marketing. Journal of Marketing Management, n. 22, 2006, p. 215-242.

MARTINS, G.A. THEÓPHILO, C. R. Metodologia da investigação científica para ciências sociais aplicadas, 2ª edição, São Paulo: Atlas, 2009.

MORGAN, R.M.; HUNT,S. D. The Commitment-Trust Theory of Relationship Marketing. Journal of Marketing, v.58, n.3, Jul., 1994, p.20-38.

NOHRIA, N. Is a network perspective a useful way of studying organizations? In NOHRIA, N.; ECLES, R. Networks and organizations: Structure, form, and action. Boston: Harvard Business School, 1992.

PERRY, M. Business clusters: an international perspective. New York: Routledge, 2005.

PALMATIER, R.W.; JARVIS, C.B; BECHKOFF, J.R. and KARDES, F.R. The Role of Customer Gratitude in Relationship Marketing. Journal of Marketing; v. 73 , September 2009, p. 1–18.

PARVATIYAR, A; SHETH, J. N. The Domain and Conceptual Foundations of Relationship Marketing. In SHETH, J.N.; PARVATIYAR. A. Handbook of Relationship Marketing. Thousand Oaks, CA: Sage Publications, 2000.

SILVA, L.A., PIMENTA, R.F., LOPES, E.L. MACHADO, E.S. Marketing de relacionamento em redes associativistas de varejo. REMark – Revista Brasileira de Marketing, São Paulo, v. 11, n. 2, p. 178-202, mai/ago. 2012.

TICHY, N.; TUSHMAN, M.; FOMBRUN, C. Social Networks analysis for organizations. Academy of Management Review, v.4, n.4, p. 507-519, 1979.

YIN, Robert K. Estudo de caso: planejamento e métodos. 4ª edição. Porto Alegre: Bookman. 2010.

# CHAPTER 6.

## PROPOSITIONS OF HOW KNOWLEDGE MANAGEMENT CAN LEAD TO A SUPERIOR PERFORMANCE IN A BUSINESS NETWORK.

### Flavio Romero Macau

Knowledge is an old concept, but it is not uncommon to be announced as one of the newest ideas for management of companies (Takeuchi, 2001). However, the issue has received more attention since the mid-1990s, given the emergence of the so called information society (Grant, 1996a; Castells, 2003). Production, acquisition, handling, retention and dissemination of knowledge became important factors for companies and for the networks in which they are embedded, leading to the increasing employment of resources to store and manage knowledge (Spender, 1996). There is ample space to define how companies perform knowledge management activities, and with what results. McKinsey and the Darmstadt University of Technology report (Takeushi, 2001) emphasize that: knowledge means different things to different people; becomes outdated quickly; is more valuable if shared (hence the importance of the network context); cannot be planned *ex ante*; has multiple dimensions. Special editions of the *Strategic Management Journal* (1996), *Management Science* (2003) and *Organization Studies* (2003, 2006) present a number of theoretical and empirical approaches, an evidence that knowledge is a comprehensive topic. To better understand its influence on business and networks it is necessary to restrict its scope. An interesting framework, adapted from Hult et al. (2007) study of supply networks, divides the topic into knowledge development and culture of competitiveness.

## 6.1. Knowledge Development

Knowledge Development is the ability to process structured information, changing actions to obtain a wider range of options. It may be conceptualized in interpersonal processes including knowledge acquisition, information distribution, shared meaning and achieved memory. This structure is based on the seminal works of Huber (1991), later adapted by a number of authors such as Szulanski (1996), Schroeder et al. (2002) and Menor, Kristal & Rosenzweig (2007).

*Knowledge Acquisition* reflects how knowledge is accessed and used, i.e. the ability to obtain information (Cohen & Levinthal, 1990; Grant, 1996b; 2002). Acquisition is made: through external activities to the company or network, such as consumer research, benchmark and competitors analysis (Conner & Prahalad, 1996; Huber, 1991); or through internal activities, such as R&D, employee (and other actors) suggestions, and experience gained with the task being performed (Schroeder *et al,* 2002; Szulanski, 1996). Knowledge is obtained from the interaction of individuals who continually review procedures, conventions and standards (Grant, 1996b). Each person has different and unequal knowledge structures that once combined enable new insights (Cohen & Levinthal, 1990). Due to cognitive limits, knowledge is acquired in a highly specialized form, and companies and networks are responsible for adding its pieces and integrate them for a concrete and productive outcome (Grant, 1996a, 1996b). Knowledge acquisition does not follow a yellow brick road: even actors who have succeeded in the task in the past may encounter problems to find and incorporate new ideas in their business and networks. *Knowledge acquisition can be seen as the ability of the network in grasping and incorporating ideas, mapping potential changes based on internal and external benchmarks.*

*Information Distribution* reflects how information is shared. The distribution (or transfer) avoids duplication of effort, capturing benefits from pockets of excellence and good ideas to replicate what works best (Szulanski, 1996). Its parameterization is difficult, since most knowledge is implicit. Thus, companies and networks which establish best ways to produce tangible knowledge, standardizing information in mapped systems by guidelines, plans, reports, charts, forecasts, routines and internal policies, tend to get important advantages in their business (Grant, 1996b). Information is distributed by rules and practices that ensure that individual experiences are passed on to other employees and actors, converting tacit and individual into explicit and collective knowledge, improving performance (Levinthal & March, 1993). The transfer is not purely rational: shared stories, myths and metaphors provide powerful means for exchange and preservation of knowledge (Nahapiet & Ghoshal, 1998). Stories full of details facilitate spreading the experience, creating patterns in which different individuals' knowledge bases connect. It can be difficult for a person to explain his personal position with rational arguments, so the more the company and the network facilitate collective interpretation, the more they will benefit from it. *Information Distribution can be seen as the ability of the network to form groups that transfer knowledge in a structured, efficient way.*

*Shared Meaning* reflects how information is understood, the process by which people translate events and share their understanding. The more one acquires knowledge, more interpretations are developed (Daft & Weick, 1984). The shared meaning is socially constructed, affected by the previous information that individuals possess and by the way a new meaning is communicated. Seldom people fully and immediately agree on a given subject, so once companies and networks are important means of coordination to the construction of meaning (Donnellon, Gray, & Bougon, 1986; Hult et al., 2007). Given differences in acquired knowledge interpretations are hardly automatic, and different skills and experiences result in the knowledge of different things, or knowledge of these same things in different ways for each person (Brown & Duguid, 2001; Conner & Prahalad, 1996). To combine the acquired and distributed information, creating a common meaning, it is necessary that the networks have overlapping areas of knowledge where the actors find intersections. Communication codes created by the group culture (e.g. jargon of R&D engineers or marketing salespeople) are valuable assets, acting as a "lubricant" that increases the exchange of information (Nahapiet & Ghoshal, 1998). This shared meaning defines which ideas are necessary and therefore preserved (Nonaka et al., 2001). Previous interpretations (pre-existing) often serve as starting point, a memory into which new knowledge is built. *Shared Meaning can be seen as the ability of the network to debate the information, discussing the most relevant events based on language and symbols internally developed.*

*Acquired memory* reflects the prior knowledge that enables new meanings to information by directing its assimilation and application (Cohen & Levinthal, 1990). What a company or network knows is difficult to specify, store and measure. Hence the difficulty in building knowledge inventories, especially in environments where change is very fast. Networks need to continually add to their knowledge base, even without knowing exactly where they are headed to. Usually when knowledge is actually needed it is already too late to start getting it from scratch; before it is needed it is very difficult to predict which parts will be vital in the future (Levinthal & March, 1993). Failure in the introduction of technologies may be the result of a mismatch between the knowledge base a company or network has and new products requirements. The key to greater efficiency is the creation of mechanisms that quickly incorporate learning, assimilating knowledge (Huber, 1991; Grant, 1996a). *Acquired memory can be seen as the ability of the network to allocate time to formally incorporate current knowledge, storing it in rules, standards, procedures and files.*

It is expected that these knowledge development elements contribute positively to the competitive advantage of companies and to the networks to which they belong, leading to a superior performance. Pisano (1994) suggests an empirical connection between cumulative experience and performance in manufacturing firms. Rosenzweig & Roth (2004) suggest that the capacity to value, assimilate and apply new knowledge results in more efficient operations. Authors like Hanvanich, Sivakumar & Hult (2006), Hult et al. (2007), Paiva et al. (2008), and Fugate, Stank & Mentzer (2009) walk a similar path, sometimes focusing on individual companies, other in supply chain networks. Therefore, knowledge development may have a positive impact on the performance of a network.

## 6.2. Culture of Competitiveness

Culture of Competitiveness is the ability to learn, create and implement actions for customer satisfaction, generating more effective results. Proposed by Hult et al. (2007) it involves resources oriented to fulfill customer needs. It may be conceptualized in interpersonal processes including learning, innovation and entrepreneurship. The effect of a the learning-innovation-performing perspective (Culture of Competitiveness) tends to be complementary to the effect of the acquire-transfer-interpret-store (Knowledge Development) perspective.

*Learning* reflects the generation of solutions that change and shape products, services and processes. Companies and networks promote their learning adjusting to conditions of the reality around them, knowingly (or not) processing large amounts of information in real time. This data must be incorporated quickly by employees and stakeholders (Uzumeri & Nembhard, 1998). Learning is a strategic resource as: it has value; it is complex and multifaceted, developing from little predictably; it is difficult to codify, leading to impacts where its causality can be ambiguous (Schroeder et al., 2002). When an activity is discontinued before it is learned, extra time and effort are spent to access the same practice again (Cohen & Levinthal, 1990). Companies and networks learn through new ways of understanding everyday problems, incorporating suggestions to their processes (Schroeder et al., 2002). Network actors (e.g. employees) continuously rearrange ideas, selecting, planning and implementing actions into increasingly complex and multifaceted process (Huber, 1991; Rosenzweig & Roth, 2004). Investing in learning leads to improvement in performance, with positive effects on productivity (Adler & Clark, 1991; Rosenzweig & Roth, 2004). *Learning can be seen as the ability of the network to solve everyday problems by incorporating the solutions to its processes.*

*Innovation* reflects the generation of ideas, the execution of something new. Its intensity depends on the ability of the company or network to explore possibilities, linking the new ideas with the pre-existing ones, improving the services that can be rendered from them (Penrose, 1959). Innovation spread possibilities that may affect profitability and business growth, impacting the performance of the company or network (Cho & Pucik, 2005). The ideas come from people, emerging from training or from on the job activities, leading to changes in the stock of existing knowledge, imperfectly transferred to companies and networks. *Innovation can be seen as the ability of the network to develop new ideas.*

*Entrepreneurship* reflects the search for and enactment of opportunities. While learning brings knowledge, and innovation generates ideas, entrepreneurship relates to implement changes. Some companies and networks convert opportunities into results faster than their peers (Richardson, 2002). This ability depends on the perception of resources availability, and the skill to combine them in different ways, in greater speed, orienting business growth (Ghoshal, Hahn, & Moran, 2002). Entrepreneurship is closely related to the adherence to a given context, as its success is linked to the results of actions implemented to a particular condition and time settings. It is this effective use of resources by network actors that generates performance, not just possessing them (Foss, 2002). Different qualities, such as courage and patience (resources typically associated with the entrepreneur), are capabilities needed to promote such guidance (Richardson, 2002). *Entrepreneurship can be seen as the ability of the network to implement change.*

It is expected that these culture of competitiveness elements contribute positively to the competitive advantage of companies and to the networks to which they belong, leading to a superior performance. More experienced, better trained actors, actively participating in new ideas generation, applied in practice to existing processes, often lead to better outcomes (Chase, Jacobs, & Aquilano, 2004; Levinthal & March, 1993; Paiva et al., 2008; Schroeder et al., 2002). Network interaction (e.g. between the company and its customers for example) is mediated by people who need an amount of autonomy to choose what is best at the moment, even opposing established rules and norms (Fitzsimmons & Fitzsimmons, 1997; Schemenner, 1999). Such "nonstandard" decisions are guided by each person's judgment, based on a set of shared values and beliefs, which will mold actions directed to customer satisfaction. Therefore, culture of competitiveness may have a positive impact on the performance of a network.

Also, as both Knowledge Development and Culture of Competitiveness may form a broader concept of knowledge management, a relationship is expected between them, with possible synergies for superior performance. From the perspective of the influence of culture on knowledge, actors involved in new experiences (learning) have new ideas (innovation), integrated in their activities (entrepreneurship). They acquire knowledge disseminated by others, building new meanings for themselves, which are integrated and stored (memory) in the company or the network. From the perspective of the influence of Knowledge Development in culture, businesses and networks that work intensively in the acquisition, transfer, sharing and storage of knowledge adjust themselves, constantly incorporating new behaviors and rituals that over time become part of their culture. Hult et al. (2007: 1039) propose that *"neither CC nor KD is enough to [alone] maximize performance. On the contrary, they complement and reinforce each other, leading to a greater strategic effect than any of them could provide alone"*. Therefore, knowledge and culture are expected to be associated with each other, having a positive multiplier effect on network performance.

## 6.3. Performance

Finding explanations for performance is an old theme, studied and developed on the strategy literature, and by no means conclusive (Combs, Crook, & Shook, 2004; Venkatraman & Ramajunam, 1986). There are several metrics, (e.g.) linked to financial indicators (ROI, ROA), operational indicators (quality, cycle time) and marketing indicators (market share, sales). Companies and networks seek better performance over time, establishing competitive advantages that consistently create superior economic value compared to competitors (Barney, 1986; Dierickx & Cool, 1989; Peteraf & Barney, 2003).

The economic value can be understood as the difference between the value that customers perceive as a benefit (B) and costs (C) to provide it. The result of (B - C) is converted into profit when the stipulated price (P) is near (or above) the perceived value (P = B). When (P <B) the customer perceives a higher added value, increasing their willingness to repurchase and disseminate the experience, leading to more customers in a movement that can be interpreted as growth (Barney & Clark, 2007). There are other variables involved in the relationship - such as capacity, inertia and the actions of competitors - but this simple model is enough to suggest the use of profitability, growth and costs as shapers of a performance construct. Classical authors of the strategy field (e.g. Ansoff, Ohmae, Penrose) focus on the growth as the main performance component. Contemporary authors (e.g. Combs, Crook, Venkatraman) focus on profitability as the main performance component. And operations literature authors (e.g. DeMeyer, Ferdows, Hayes, Upton) often focus costs as determinant for performance.

Therefore, costs, profitability and growth can be performance proxies, and an important research topic would be to determine whether, how and why Knowledge Development, Culture of Competitiveness and their interaction may lead to superior performance in business networks

# References

Adler, Paul S.; & Clark, Kim B. (1991) Behind the Learning Curve: A sketch of the learning process. Management Science, 37 (3), March.

Barney, Jay B. (1986). Strategic factor markets: expectations, luck and business strategy. Management Science, 32 (10), October.

Barney, J. B.; Clark, D. N. (2007). Creating and sustaining competitive advantage. New York: Oxford University Press.

Brown, J.; & Duguid, P. (2001) Structure and Spontaneity: knowledge and organization. In: Nonaka, Ikujiro; & Teece, David J. Managing industrial knowledge. London: Sage.

Brown, Timothy. (2006). Confirmatory factor analysis: for applied research. New York: Guilford Publications.

Chase, Richard B.; Jacobs, Robert F.; & Aquilano, Nicholas, J. (2004). Operations management for competitive advantage (10th ed.). New York: McGraw-Hill.

Cho, Hee-Jae; Pucik, Vladimir. (2005). Relationship between innovativeness, quality, growth, profitability, and market value. Strategic Management Journal, 26, 555–575.

Cohen, Wesley M.; & Levinthal, Daniel A. (1990). Absorptive capacity: a new perspective on learning and innovation. Administrative Science Quarterly, 35 (1), March.

Combs, James; Crook, Toledo; Shook, Carole (2004). Dimension organizational performance and its implications for strategic management research. In: Ketchen, David J.; Bergh, Donald D. Research methodology in strategy and management. San Diego: Elsevier.

Conner, Kathleen; & Prahalad, C. K. (1996). A resource-based theory of the firm: knowledge versus opportunism. Organization Science, 7 (5), September-October.

Daft, Richard L.; & Weick, K. E. (1984). Toward a model of organizations as interpretation systems. Academy of Management Review, 9, 284-295.

Dierickx, Ingemar; & Cool, Karel. (1989). Asset stock accumulation and sustainability of competitive advantage. Management Science, 35 (12), 1504-1511.

Donnellon, A.; & Gray, B.; Bougon, M. G. (1986). Communication, meaning, and Organized Action. Administrative Science Quarterly, 31, 43-55.

Fitzsimmons, James A.; & Fitzsimmons, Mona J. (1997). Service management : operations, strategy, and information technology. Palatino (CA): McGraw-Hill.

Foss, N. J. (2002). Edith Penrose and strategic management. In: Pitelis, Christos. The growth of the firm: the legacy of Edith Penrose. Oxford: Oxford University Press.

Frohlicha, Markham T.; Westbrook, Roy. (2002). Demand chain management in manufacturing and services. Journal of Operations Management, 20, 729–745.

Fugate, Brian S.; Stank, Theodore P.; Mentzer, John T. (2009). Linking improved knowledge management to operational and organizational performance. JOM, 27, 247–264.

Ghoshal, Sumantra; Hahn, Martin; Moran, Peter. (2002). Management competence, firm growth and economic progress. In: Pitelis, Christos. The growth of the firm: the legacy of Edith Penrose. Oxford: Oxford University Press.

Grant, Robert M. (1996a). Toward a knowledge-based theory of the firm. Strategic Management Journal, 17, Winter Special Issue.

Grant, Robert M. (1996b). Prospering in Dynamically-competitive Environments: organizational capability as knowledge integration. Organization Science, 7 (4).

Grant, Robert (2002). The knowledge-based view of the firm. In: Choo, Chun; Bontis, Nick. The strategic management of intellectual capital and organizational. New York: Oxford.

Haksever, Sengis; Render, Barry; Russel, Roberta S.; & Murdick, Robert G. (2000). Service management and operations. Upper Saddle River (NJ):Prentice Hall.

Hanvanich, Sangphet; Sivakumar, K.; Hult, G. T. M. (2006). The relationship of learning and memory with organizational performance: the moderating role of turbulence. Journal of the Academy of Marketing Science, 34 (4), 600-612.

Huber, G. P. (1991). Organizational Learning: the contributing processes and the literatures. Organization Science, 2 (1), February.

Hult, G. T. M.; Ketchen, David J.; & Nichols, Ernest. L. Jr. (2003). Organizational learning as a strategic resource in supply management. Journal of Operations Management, 21.

Hult, G. T. M.; Ketchen, David J.; & Arrfelt, Mathias. (2007). Strategic supply chain management. Strategic Management Journal, 28, 1035–1052.

Kline, Rex B. (2004). Principles and Practice of Structural Equation Modeling. New York: Guilford Press.

Levinthal, D.; & March, J. G. (1993). The myopia of learning. Strategic Management Journal, 14, Winter.

Mathe, Hervé; & Shapiro, Roy D. (1993). Integrating service strategy in the manufacturing company. London: Chapman & Hall.

Menor, Larry J.; Kristal, M. Murat; & Rosenzweig, Eve D. (2007). Examining the Influence of operational intellectual capital on capabilities and performance. Manufacturing & Service Operations Management, 9 (4), 559-578, Fall.

Nahapiet, Janine; & Ghoshal, Sumantra. (1998). Social capital, intellectual capital, and the organizational advantage. Academy of Management Review, 23 (2), April.

Paiva, Eli L.; Roth, Aleda V.; & Fernsterseifer, Jaime E. (2008). Organizational knowledge and the manufacturing strategy process. Journal of Operations Management, 26, 115-132.

Penrose, Edith T. (1959). The theory of the growth of the firm. New York: John Wiley &Sons.

Peteraf, M. A.; & Barney, J. B. (2003). Unraveling the resource-based tangle. Managerial and Decision Economics, 24 (4), 309-323.

Pisano, Gary P. (1994). Knowledge integration and the locus of learning. Strategic Management Journal, 15, 85-100.

Richardson, G.B. (2002). Mrs Penrose and neoclassical theory. In: Pitelis, Christos. The growth of the firm: the legacy of Edith Penrose. Oxford: Oxford University Press.

Schemenner, Roger W. (1999). Service operations management. Hemel Hempstead (UK): Prentice Hall.

Schroeder, Roger G.; Bates, Kimberly A.; & Junttila, Mikko. (2002). A resource-based view of manufacturing strategy and the relationship to manufacturing performance. SMJ, 23.

Sengupta, Kaushik; Heiser, Daniel R.; Cook, Lori S. (2006). Manufacturing and service supply chain performance: a comparative analysis. Journal of Supply Chain, 42 (4), 5-16.

Spender, J. C. (1996). Making knowledge the basis of a dynamic theory of the firm. Strategic Management Journal, 17, 45-62, Winter Special Issue.

Szulanski, Gabriel. (1996). Exploring internal stickiness: impediments to the transfer of best practice within the firm. Strategic Management Journal, 17, Winter Special Issue.

Takeushi, H. (2001). Towards a universal management concept of knowledge. In: Nonaka, Ikujiro; Teece, David J. Managing industrial knowledge. London: Sage.

Uzumeri, Mustafa; & Nembhard, David. (1998). A population of learners: a new way to measure organizational learning. Journal of Operations Management, 16, 515-528.

Venkatraman, N.; Ramanujam, Vasudevan. (1986). Measurement of business performance in strategy research: a comparison of approaches. Academy of Management Review, 1 (4).

Zander, Udo; & Kogut, Bruce. (1995). Knowledge and the speed of the transfer and imitation of organizational capabilities: an empirical test. Organization Science, 6 (1), January.

# Chapter 7.

## Brand image in a networked society: the Harley-Davidson and Buell case

Celso A. Rimoli;
Léo Eduardo P. Noronha;
Eduardo Clemente Alves.

**Summary.**

Among the various trends currently impacting the business world, two stand out: the fact that society is increasingly organized in networks and the high rate of innovation that characterizes its survival. As a result of this, in the networked society, aspects related to brand tend to make a product or service more competitive than its own quality, which is a fundamental attribute, but that does not differentiate from the offer of competitors. In this context, the purpose of this chapter is to analyze how aspects of innovation and networks affect the image of global brands. To achieve this goal the Harley-Davidson and Buell brands of Harley-Davidson Motor Company were examined. The results indicated greater importance of networks to the former brand's key actors and innovation to the latter.

## 7. 1.Introduction

This chapter addresses how innovations, products and messages spread across business networks. Its context is placed by Rouen and Fanhagmer (2000), who found that the intensification of technology and innovation in a society organized in global networks are making brands more important than the quality of the respective products to differentiate the offer of companies in the market. Most importantly in this process is the image that consumers build on the brands. Thus, this chapter aims at analyzing how aspects of innovation and networks affect the image of global brands. It was necessary to find objects of study compatible with this question, and after extensive search, we decided to examine the Harley-Davidson (HD) and Buell brands, from Harley-Davidson Motor Company. The choice of these brands was because a secondary research indicated that HD presents aspects of networks such as Harley owners group (HOG) while Buell shows more innovative features.

The work was performed as an in-depth investigation through multiple case study research strategy (Yin, 2010). The proposed objective and the examination of the secondary information on the two brands led to the elaboration of the following propositions:

1. Innovation characterizes Buell brand more intensely

2. Networks characterize HD brand more intensely.

3. Innovation has had great importance in HD brand's history and strengthens it to the present day.

## 7.2. Literature review

Sections 2.1 and 2.2 of the review, on networks and innovation, adopt the contents of the essay of Rimoli and Giglio (2009) to the theme ending up with a conceptual model proposition.

### 7.2.1 Business Networks

To understand the theories that characterize networks it is required to present their central concepts. As Kempe, Kleinberg and Tardos (2005) state, networks are representations of relations and interactions between individuals and groups, playing an important role as a means of dissemination of information, ideas, influences, products and services. Ebers and Jarillo (1997) define networks as a set of connections called nodes, which are the basic units of networks and represent the gathering of actors such as suppliers, customers, competitors, government, research institutes, press, etc.

As Hakansson and Snehota (1995) establish, the structure of a node comprises three items: actors, resources and activities. Among the most important resources some authors (Gulati; Gargiulo, 1999; Uzzi, 1997) have highlighted the embeddedness, whose basic idea is the social and economic intertwining between the actors that simultaneously imposes limits of mutual behavior and develop other resources, including social capital.

According to Tichy, Tushman and Fombrun (1979), the approach of social networks conceives organizations in society as a system of objects (individuals, groups or companies) united by various relationships. Not all objects are directly linked, but some are by multiple relationships. Salancik (1995), states that networks are built from interactions among individuals and organizations enabling the emergence of certain structures. In them, it is important to consider whether there are actors with more relationships than others (centrality), if each network member can be contacted by the others (density), the size of the network, etc. Thus the social stream of networks search for substantiation and investigates the political, historical, cultural and social fields to understand the business networks. For example, in their works, Sobel and Piore (1984) and Putnam (1996) have shown interest in issues related to trust, cultural identity, social interaction, historical prerogatives and territoriality of the phenomena. To achieve such results it should be noted that the success of networks is in the management of conflicts and individual interests. And the control of this management ranges from strict measures, as in the case of an existing central actor, to even extremely democratic decision dynamics..

In this context, as highlighted by Castells (2000) and Ozcan (2004), there is a process of transformation of a society based on markets to a network society, in which the actors migrate from individual positions and decisions to interdependence and cooperation ones, in their connections within the network. Such transformation includes a different logic for the exchange processes, changing from transaction into relational bases as an alternative to discrete or positional transactions (Castells, 2000; Dwyer; Schurr; Oh, 1987; Klein, 2003; Ozcen, 2004).

## 7.2.2 Innovation

According to Mariano (2004) innovation has moved from a purely technical vision to a concept of innovation that covers any knowledge that adds value to the development and commercialization of products and services and to the management of organizations. Moreira and Queiroz (2007) stated that various authors have proposed various innovation classifications such as technological, organizational, product and process, incremental and radical among others. Lemos (1999) affirmed that incremental innovations involve improvements to existing products, processes and methods, featuring evolutionary changes in a condition known as *customer pull*. Differently, radical innovations involve the use of inventions or laboratory results on search for profitable commercial applications. The author argues that radical innovations usually unfold in brand new products or processes or in a novel way of organizing the production site. So, they can break the current technological standards, giving origin to new organizations, industries and markets. For these reasons, they characterize situations known as *technology push*.

From this characterization, John, Weiss and Dutta (1999) and Mohr, Sengupta and Slater (2005) argued that marketing needs to be adapted so that it can deal effectively with very innovative situations. The more a sector is characterized by incremental innovations, more conventional the marketing approach should be. At the other extreme, the more companies offer radically innovative products and services to the market, more its marketing tools should be adapted to these conditions. As Hills and Sarin (2003) note, the greater the degree of innovation involved in goods and services, the harder it will be to understand the needs of consumers by traditional methods.

### 7.2.3 Innovation and networks influencing the identity and brand image

Aaker (1996), Kapferer (1992), Seguela (1982) among others have identified several different elements that form brands, but in this chapter the focus was directed only to the identity, communication and brand image, which are shown in Figure 1.

Brand identity is the set of attributes that characterize the essence of a product or organization for which the organization would like to be recognized by its audiences. According to Kapferer (2004) brand identity is composed of a set of attributes defined in six dimensions: physical environment, personality, culture, relationship, reflection and mind set. As for Aaker (1996) it is the set of associations that gives sense, meaning and purpose to a particular brand, forging unique and non-transferable characteristics. To this author, identity is what the brand wants to perform and involves a promise made to customers by members of the organization according to four dimensions: product, organization, person and symbol, which are detailed in 12 attributes.

The second element of Figure 1, the media, addresses the issue of dissemination, which is crucial since the brand exists only in so far as it is recognized by the consumer. In order for the physical and psychological identity to happen, it is necessary that the brand is offered to the target groups and accepted by them. The marketing area should concentrate efforts not only on clear and consistent definition of a strong identity for brands, but also on developing a communication mix able to spread it out. As stated by Kapferer (1992), the brand, by setting out products and services among of other values, depends on the communication to be known and recognized. Thus the brand communication is the transfer process leading identity to brand image.

The third element of Figure 1, brand image is the result of the mental synthesis, made by target audiences, of all the signals emitted by the brand, such as name, visual symbols, products, advertisements, sponsorships etc. To Koubaa (2008) it comes from the mental configuration and analytical process of individuals, as their formation is subject to external and internal factors to them. The construction of any brand image requires receivers interpreting and decoding the set of signals emitted by the brand (Kotler and Keller, 2006). In the decoding process the receiver contributes heavily to the outcome, that is, there is a part of building the brand image that does not depend on the realized stimulus, but on the conceptualization process of the receiver. The result is the distinction between identity that the brand projects into the market - and the image perceived by it - the one that target audiences build from contacts they established with the brand. Therefore, brand management will be most effective the more it can reduce to a minimum the differences between what the company sends as the brand (its identity) and what their public perceive of it (its image).

So at the end of the diffusion process, there is the image of the brand, which for Barich and Kotler (1991, p. 95), *"is the sum of beliefs, attitudes and impressions that a person or group has on an object ... Impressions can be true or false, real or imaginary. Right or wrong, the image guides and shapes the behavior of individuals."* In short, the currently dominant view in the literature is that the brand management strategies must be consistent over time and space in order to produce more favorable brand associations (Keller, 2008). This consistency results from the degree of proximity between the identity and brand image (Matthiesen; Phau, 2010).

Figure 7.1 also brings the influence of innovation and networks on brand building, two light blue bands accompanying the formation of image process described. It is proposed that the emergence of innovations affects the brand image formation process, and its monitoring should be effective. Innovation aspects involved in this dynamic are reflected in needs and desires still not aware by consumers and in unprecedented solutions that address old desires and needs. In addition, it is considered that the impact of innovation happen in a networked society and it must take into account the structural features (centrality, level of aggregation, etc.) and behavioral features (trust, commitment, cooperation, etc.) of the actors.

It is understood that these aspects act since the construction of identity, through communication directed to target groups, and influence the way they receive the signals, forming the brand image.

**Figure 7.1. Innovation, networks and the shaping brand image**

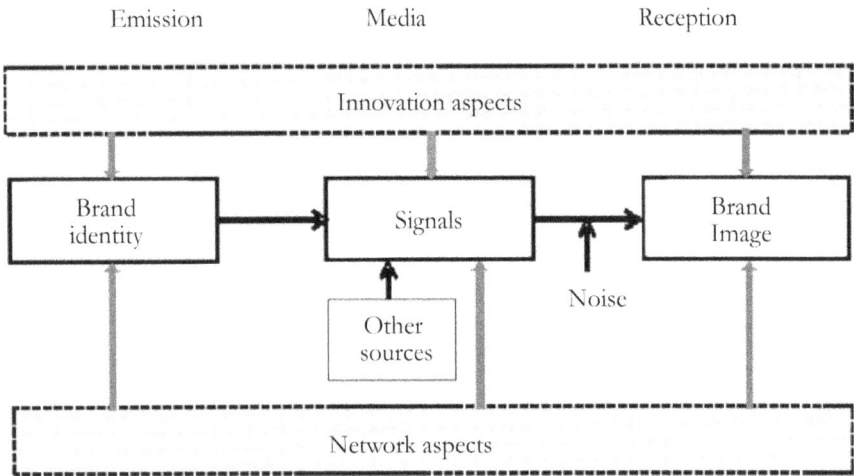

Source: The authors, based on Kapferer (1992).

## 7.3. Methodological considerations

This work is descriptive, but also exploratory as it seeks to deepen the characterization of a phenomenon. It is the study of a current phenomenon in which the boundaries between it and its context are not very clear. The unit of analysis is the brand image and it was used the literal replication, in search of consistent results, using two brands of the same company (Yin, 2010).

The data collected came from three sources: secondary, primary of informal character (observation) and primary of formal character (six in-depth interviews with owners of the bikes and one with the representative of Izzo Group), featuring a data triangulation with multiple sources of evidence. Three motorcycle owners were identified for each brand, distributed at the beginning, middle and end of the respective age groups described in paragraphs 4.1.3 and 4.1.4. In addition, they all already had an HD or Buell motorcycle for at least one year at the time of the interview.

The analysis of this work was based on the general analytical strategy 'based on theoretical propositions', making use of specific analytical pattern matching technique (Yin, 2010). Cross-case synthesis (sequential results of questions for each brand individually and between the two brands for each question) were also performed, including full cases and theory and looking for patterns and differences. We also sought to meet the validity criteria by regarding the triangulation of data, linking and convergence of evidence.

## 7.4. Presentation and analysis of the collected data

 This section presents the data collected and the analyzes carried out as the proposed line of discussion.

### 7.4.1 Secondary information: The company and the two brands.

The emergence and consolidation of HD Company had been highlighted by various historical events during the twentieth century in America, and it is one of the reasons of patriotism attribute associated with the brand in that country. Thus, in 1916 the General John J. 'Black Jack 'Pershing went, in an HD motorcycle, to capture Pancho Villa during the Mexican Revolution. In World War I, the Americans entered the rugged German territory for the first time with a soldier riding a HD. After peace was restored, the HD back on track in 1921 and it became the first team to win a speed race over 160 Km / h. Then in World War II the company specialized in building military motorcycles, some of them equipped with sidecars coupled with automatic weapons.

Years after the end of World War II, the American market was rekindled and many who had fought the war became the main buyers of HD brand as wanted to experience it as civilians. From 1953 the company strengthened further with the failure of the Indian competitor, which became the only American manufacturer of motorcycles. The following year, with the film The Wild One starring Marlon Brando, the image of motorcyclists and the HD brand gained new contours as they were seen as out-of-law and troublemakers. After all those events, it has been said that the 1950s were taken by the spirit of HD motorcycles.

In the early 1960s, even before the full recovery of the American market, large Japanese competitors arrived such as Honda and Kawasaki, focusing on the segment of small models. At the end of that decade, the HD Company was acquired by American Machine & Foundry Co (AMF), a product for recreation company. Due to their rapid growth plans, the quality of HD bikes deteriorated. At the same time, Japanese manufacturers entered the main HD segment of large motorcycles. The crisis reached its peak in the early 1980s when the company almost went bankrupt. Then the directors, including the grandson of the founder, resumed the property of the company and gave priority to product quality and attention to the consumer. Internally, the board offered to employees of the factory of Pennsylvania stock options, and for producing well, delegated to them the decision to close production lines with bad operation. Externally, executives sought to listen to customers and offer them better products by the brand community, the HOG.

With these measures employees rescued the feeling of being artists who produced rare jewels, greatly increasing their identification with the company. And consumers responded very positively, generating increasing profits, valued stocks and large increase of brand prestige. HD bikes now bring the design and the engineering conception back from a glorious past.

Concurrently in 1983 the engineer and competition pilot Erik Buell, employee for four years in the HD company decided to build competition motorcycles that vied the market with the Japanese and the Italian, founding the Buell Motorcycle Company. In 1993 Buell started a successful partnership with HD, and in 1998 was fully merged into the parent company. From that time on the Buell brand started to take advantage of all the technology and credibility of the century brand. At the unit, there are currently producing around 10,000 bikes a year, as well as parts, accessories and special clothing.

The manufacture of HD and Buell product is completely made in the USA, being marketed in Brazil exclusively by Izzo Group. Dealerships and HD and Buell stores are arms of Izzo group and they are not separate companies. It's a simple business setting, closer to a traditional supply chain than a business network. Still, the relationship between the actors indicates two-way flow of at least one of three elements: goods, services and information.

### 7.4.1.1 Harley Owners Group (HOG)

One of the unique aspects of the company HD is the involvement of its staff and dealerships with its customers, as evidenced by the flourishing existence of HOG. More than 250,000 HD motorcycle owners belong to one of its more than 800 Chapters. Its members receive a bimonthly newsletter and participate with the family of motorcycle riding as well as in meetings and breakfasts, on a monthly or weekly basis, all sponsored by the company and by the concessionaires. There is also a subgroup called Ladies of Harley (LOH), composed of women which correspond to 10% of HD owners.

In the US, the tours are traditionally organized by the HOG to visit to Daytona Beach and the city of Milwaukee, where the company was born. In Brazil, the tours are organized by the different Chapters having as destinations different touristic points in the cities in their respective states such as Búzios (RJ), Florianópolis (SC), etc. The HD employees, from engineering management to the simplest positions, have participated in HOG meetings. So they know their customers personally and can collect suggestions and strengthen ties.

### 7.4.1.2 The HD brand

It was found that the HD brand expresses experience, attitude, lifestyle and identifies their owners, translating values such as individuality and personal freedom, which refers to being free from both physical confinement and from dominant social values. Another important value is masculinity (as in the film *The wild one*, already mentioned). The HD is the biggest, heaviest, noisy and vigorous bike on roads. There are items of clothing that reinforce these values and thus the brand identity is intertwined with the very history of the company.

The HD brand is classic, traditional and of national character, besides its authenticity, sobriety and elitism in relation to the market. And it is identified as element of fixed value, timeless, a rare gem, valuable both for company personnel and to consumers of the brand. HD bikes are classic and bring with them the spirit of past times to its user. They have functional design and even though are less technologically updated than competitors, this feature do not compromise the product's purposes.

However, it is important to emphasize that part of the traditionalism that today characterizes the HD brand is due to long lasting innovations. For example, the engines in "V", which today are the basis of traditional model HD Custom were considered innovative when they were released. These bikes can be customized to the style of each client, with the available accessories. Thus, at different times in its history, innovations accounted for attributes that today add value the brand and make it classic. In addition to technical innovations, they also involved design (drop-shaped tank, seat saddle-shaped, round headlight, long wheelbase, riding position with good ergonomics for long trips). Figure 7.2, below illustrates the motorcycle and the respective HD brand.

**Figure 7.2. Harley-Davidson Heritage Classic model.**

**Source: Harley-Davidson Brazil.**

The involvement of 'harleiros', as the owners of the HD brand are called in Brazil, is closer and more engaged than it occurs to owners of Japanese motorcycles and their brands. They focus on functional, technological and performance benefits, such as digital equipment, reverse gear, high speed and quieter engines. Unlike HD motorcycle owners are more linked to emotional benefits and self-expressive.

HD owners form a primarily male audience (about 90%) in the range of 36-59 years, they are successful people professionally, they belong to high and upper-middle classes and show satisfaction and loyalty to the product and brand. The vast majority intends to purchase another bike HD when changing the current. Thus, having a relationship with a strong brand is something satisfying and rewarding, as is the connection to the HOG group that shares personal values and lifestyle.

Negative points of the brand are observed in some weaknesses identified at the Izzo Group, related to its participation as an intermediary between the manufacturer and consumers, as well as regarding its post-sales services.

### 7.4.1.3 The Buell brand

Despite belonging to the same company, the Buell brand brings only the strength of the manufacturer and users give greater value to the product characteristics. The research revealed that Buell brand identity focuses on an innovative, extravagant and youthful character. Buell motorcycles stand out in quality, technology and performance attributes and they differ from HD, and competitors mainly by the attribute innovation in design, in mechanical solutions and in technology upgrades. The vocation to innovate for all Buell models was built around the so-called 'technology trilogy': low weight, frame rigidity and mass centralization.

Examples of such innovations are: exhaust placed under the motorcycle, instead of at its side; fuel tank inside the aluminum frame, with 16.7 liters. In the traditional tank's place, it is the air filter and the body of the injection, which can be seen through the translucent acrylic cover. As a result, the rigid chassis reduces the flexibility but increases the motorcycle stability, especially on rough roads. Other technical solutions are: it obtains the lowest possible weight of all the components not supported by springs, allowing the tires to maintain constant contact with the track. And the brake Zero Torsion Load (ZTL) a system in which the brake disc is fixed to the rim of the front wheel and not at the outside of the central hub, which makes the braking safer for not twisting the brake disc and reducing in three kilograms the weight on the front of the bike. Figure 7.3 below shows the motorcycle and Buell brand.

Figure 7.3. Buell City Cross model.

Source: Buell Brazil.

Buell owners are almost entirely men of the upper and middle-upper classes, aged between 25 and 35 years, professionally successful, and most of them indicated low intention to acquire another Buell when changing their current bike. Regarding the relationship with the consumer, the Buell brand reveals dynamic mood, vitality, sense of opportunity and superficiality, because of the speed with which this market evolves. Competition from Japanese motorcycles, with high technology is strong, so maybe because of that the HD company has acquired Buell. With this action, the company went on to compete in the market segment in which Japanese motorcycles operate.

### 7.4.2 Primary information: interviews and observation

First to point out are the similarities between the two brands as the fact that both value the sense of freedom, as well as how much each type of consumer is adept of its brand. However, this sense of freedom is founded on different bases: the HD brand enshrines freedom of confinement and social conventions, but it is adept of group activities (HOG activities with family and breakfasts in dealerships). In contrast, the freedom to Buell is based on sportsmanship and individual freedom to get out and explore places without wives or girlfriends.

Other distinctions involve the solidity and the sense of permanence of HD brand, with its classic design and technical concepts that build on what was developed in the 1950s. Its personality is robust and genuine, and the bike was designed to run primarily on roads and users are predominantly men between 36 and 59 years. By contrast, Buell adherents are almost all men aged between 25 and 35 years and the group is less numerous and more recent - while the HD brand is centenary, the Buell brand was started in 1983. But, as for the `sister brand', Buell owners are quite adherent to Buell brand attributes. These include innovation and technological upgrading of the bikes, which are more suitable for driving in urban areas. Attributes such as trust and cooperation among Buell owners exist but are restricted to the exchange of information about the products and their problems, being thinner than the HD brand. Something that helps to consolidate the Buell brand and is valuable to the owners is the reputation of the manufacturer that the brand carries.

As for the propositions formulated based on secondary information, all the respondents confirmed them. The first states what aspects of innovation affect more intensely the Buell brand. They cited design and technological innovations such as low center of gravity, the brake system, etc. The brand traditionally brings only the HD engine. Users of Buell appreciate innovations and the general idea is that this brand is distinct from HD brand: as one of the interviewees said "it came to innovate".

The second proposition says that aspects of networks affect the HD brand more and it also showed a high level of agreement of respondents because users appreciate the exchange of information, cooperation, group tours with family (HOG), the breakfasts at dealerships, etc. Buell Respondents recognized these attributes to the HD brand, but stressed that there is also confidence among users of the Buell brand.

And finally the third proposition says that innovation was very important in a given historical context of the HD brand, which favors its strength today. The agreement was also strong, but more intense among users of HD brand, who know their history better than the Buell brand users. We emphasize the response of the representative of Izzo Group, illustrating the truth of this proposition "knowing the historical evolution of Harley, I realize that innovations like the tank in drop form, the long wheelbase, the 'V' engine , the use of chrome, etc. were the creators of the HD Custom style, which is copied by the competition".

## 7. 5. Final considerations

This study sought to know how aspects of innovation and networks affect the image of global brands. The results showed strong adherence between the collection of secondary and primary data, which allowed consistent response to the goal formulated as an examination of the three propositions applied to the object of study (HD and Buell brands).

The evidence collected indicated a traditional commercialization structure instead of a network regarding HD and Buell motorcycles in Brazil, consisting of three main actors the Izzo Group (commercialization, dealerships and technical assistance), the HD customers and its HOG subgroup and Buell customers. However, the HOG might be considered as a network and that could be examined in future research.

In addition, aspects of innovation, such as design and technology upgrades affect more intensely the Buell brand (Proposition 1) and aspects of networking, such as trust, cooperation and relationship affect more HD brand (Proposition 2). It was also evident that while aspects of innovation are not important for HD brand today, they were fundamental for the consolidation of the brand in the 1950s, when the model HD Custom emerged (Proposition 3), one of the references of the brand that is imitated by competitors.

Something that was not explicit in interview questions, but that appeared during the collection and analysis of data is that the Harley-Davidson company might use the strategy to target the owners of Buell to becoming HD owners in the long run. In support of this assertion, there is some evidence. Firstly, the fact of the sequential age ranges Buell owners are between 25 and 35 years; the HD are between 36 and 59 years. Secondly, although the consumer profile of the two brands is distinguished, it can be considered sequential. Specifically, the young tend to seek more innovation and excitement and be more individualistic (Buell attributes), but as they get older, they would value stability, tradition and group activities (HD attributes). Thirdly, the Buell buyers in general tend not to buy a new bike of the same brand, while the HD owners do so. These reflections could be the subject of another study, continuing to this.

Regarding the implications of the results of this research to understand the formation of the brand image and contribute to its management we could say that this work has brought some progress. The confirmation of the applied propositions highlighted some points: they are complementary motorcycle brands in the sense that they were targeted to different but sequential consumer segments, at least in characteristics such as age range and socioeconomic status. Findings such as innovation being prevalent with the Buell brand, networks with HD and also innovation being fundamental for the strength of the latter nowadays, indicates the importance of these aspects in their development and success.

We believe that the data and analysis endorse an explicit consideration of the aspects of innovation, and networks in the formation and management of brand image in general. Although it is a descriptive-exploratory research of qualitative character, there was great consistency, convergence and enchainment of evidence that bring robustness as to the results obtained and meet the validity criteria presented by Yin (2010). Nevertheless, we suggest the replication of this study with other brands and also other related qualitative and quantitative researches.

# References

AAKER, D. Building strong brands. New York: The Free Press, 1996.

BARICH, H.; KOTLER, P. A framework for marketing image management. Sloan Management Review, v. 32, p. 94-104, 1991.

CASTELLS, M. Materials for an exploratory theory of the network society. British Journal of Sociology, v. 51, n. 1, jan/fev, p. 5-24, 2000.

DWYER, F. R.; SCHURR, P. H.; OH, S. Developing buyer-seller relationships. Journal of Marketing; v. 51; p. 11-27, abr. 1987.

EBERS, M.; JARILLO, J. The construction, forms and consequences of industry networks. International Studies of Management and Organizations, v. 27, n. 4. p. 3-21, 1997.

GULATI, R.; GARGIULO, M. Where do interorganizational networks come from? American Journal of Sociology. v. 104, n. 5, p.1439-1493, mar. 1999.

HAKANSSON, H.; SNEHOTA, I. Developing relationships in business networks. London: T. J. Press, 1995.

HILLS, S. B.; SARIN, S. From market driven to market driving: an alternate paradigm for marketing. Journal of Marketing Theory and Practice. v. 11, n. 3, p. 13-23, 2003.

JOHN, G.; WEISS, A.; DUTTA, S. Marketing in technology intensive markets: toward a conceptual framework. Journal of Marketing, Special Issue, v. 63, p.78-91, 1999.

KAPFERER, J. N. New strategic brand management. 3. ed. London: Kogan Pages, 2004.

KAPFERER, J. N. Strategic brand management. New York: Free Press, 1992.

KELLER, K. L. Strategic Brand Management. 3. ed. Upper Saddle River: Pearson, 2008.

KEMPE, D.; KLEINBERG, J.; TARDOS, E. Influential nodes in a diffusion model for social networks. Proceedings of the 32nd International Colloquium on Automata, Languages and Programming. ICALP, 2005.

KLEIN, M. V. Identificação do nível de relacionamento entre a claro digital e seus clientes corporativos. 2003. Dissertação (Mestrado em Administração). Universidade Federal do Rio Grande do Sul. Porto Alegre, 2003.

KOTLER, P.; KELLER, K. L. Administração de marketing. 12 ed. São Paulo: Pearson Prentice Hall, 2006.

KOUBAA, Y. Country of origin, brand image perception and brand image structure. Asia Pacific Journal of Marketing and Logistics, v. 20, n. 2, p. 139-155, 2008.

LEMOS, C. Inovação na era do conhecimento. In: LASTRES, H.; ALBAGLI, S. Informação e globalização na era do conhecimento. Rio de Janeiro: Campus, 1999.

MARIANO, S. Gestão da inovação: Uma Abordagem Integrada. Relatório técnico. Universidade Federal Fluminense, 2004.

MATTHIESEN, I.; PHAU, I.; Brand image inconsistencies of luxury fashion brands. Journal of Fashion Marketing and Management, v. 14, n. 2, p. 202-218, 2010.

MOREIRA, D.; QUEIROZ, A. C. Inovação: conceitos fundamentais. In: MOREIRA, D.; QUEIROZ, A. (Orgs.). Inovação Organizacional e Tecnológica. São Paulo: Thomson, 2007.

OZCAN, K. Consumer-to-Consumer interactions in a networked society: Word-Of-Mouth Theory, Consumer Experiences, and Network Dynamics. University of Michigan United States. Michigan, Ago, 2004.

PIORE, M.; SOBEL, C. F. The second industrial divide possibilities for prosperity. Nova York: Basic Books, 1984.

PUTNAN, R. D. Comunidade e democracia: A experiência da Itália Moderna. Rio de Janeiro: Fundação Getúlio Vargas, 1996.

RIMOLI, C. A.; GIGLIO, E. M. Contribuição das teorias de redes e de inovação para marketing. In: Anais do XXXIII Encontro da ANPAD, São Paulo, ANPAD, 2009.

RUÃO, T.; FARHANGMER, M. A Imagem da marca: Análise das funções de representação e apelo no marketing das marcas. Um Estudo de Caso. Actas do I Seminário de Marketing Estratégico e Planejamento. Escola de Economia e Gestão, Universidade do Minho, Portugal. 2000.

SALANCIK, G. R. Wanted: a good network theory of organization. Administrative Science Quarterly, v. 40, n. 2, p. 345-349, 1995.

SEGUELA, J. Hollywood lave plus blanc. France: Flammarion, 1982.

TICHY, N.; TUSHMAN, M.; FOMBRUN, C. Social networks analysis for organizations. Academy of Management Review, v. 4, n. 4, p. 507-519, 1979.

UZZI, B. Social structure and competition in interfirm networks: the paradox of embeddedness. Administrative Science Quarterly, v. 42, n. 1, p. 35-67, mar. 1997.

YIN, Robert K. Estudo de caso: planejamento e métodos. 4. ed. Porto Alegre: Bookman, 2010.

# Chapter 8.
## When a Cooperative Network loses its Mission: The Example of Housing Cooperatives.

Ernesto M. Giglio,
José Roberto Gamba,
Augusto C. D'Arruda,
Maria Carolina Arruda

**Resume**

The chapter carries out a raid on the principles of the cooperative collective action, particularly in housing cooperatives, presenting it as a social, political and economic movement, able to offer a housing alternative, different from normal market supply pattern. The cooperative principle is the rule of community work, placing the common goal (the condition of purchasing a home), cooperation and commitment above other interests. In addition to this more economical prospect of purchasing a material good, the cooperative promotes the ethics of equality and justice. It happens that the Brazilian housing cooperatives, driven by the government and then abandoned by the government, have chosen to follow a path of survival by adopting competitive models market, losing their social mission. The research revealed a position of competition with contractors and other government housing programs. Interviewed actors place cooperatives in this competitive perspective. In the discussion of the results and comments, there is discussion on the consequences for this strategic decision, in view of the growing interest and development of collective actions, such as partnerships, cooperation networks, business networks, fair trade networks, implementation of networks public policy; walking along with new conceptions of a networked society.

## 8.1 Introduction

During the eighteenth and nineteenth centuries, facing the advance of capitalism and its consequences for much of the population, there were movements of new forms of production and consumption that were ruled by ideals of social justice and solidarity. More recently, in the last quarter of the twentieth century there was a reinvigoration of these ideals, which resulted in the search for alternatives for solutions against poverty, exclusion, unemployment, homelessness and the individualistic culture, with buoyed initiatives in ideals of equality, cooperation and solidarity. Cooperativism is part of this movement, with current developments such as the voluntary market and the solidarity economy.

The cooperativism in its economic solidarity manifestation is characterized according to a set of principles and values of the social group that originates, which means that each collective manifestation has its own characteristics. In this sense, cooperativism is a superior alternative to capitalism, because it includes the specific characteristics of the group, which facilitates commitment, resulting in quality of work, life and an identity to the actors (Singer, 2005 and 2008).

Adopting the cooperative principles and the statements of the networked society approach (Castells, 1999), the chapter discusses the ways of working of Brazilian housing cooperatives, their continuity strategies, having as the model of collective action network proposal to maintain and develop the organizations of cooperative construction.

A research was conducted by collecting data from government secretaries, directors, managers and technicians involved in the production of cooperative construction and the results indicated that investigated housing cooperatives abdicated collective action and networking, adopting a competition isolated position. As a result, they were forced to offer products according to market demand, which means houses also for the middle and upper class, as well as leisure villas and properties for investment.

The single strand of cooperativism was found in relations between representatives of cooperatives and the actual members, with signs of governance, transparency, interdependence and commitment.

## 8.2 The cooperative theme in civil construction

According to Hart (2006) and Prahalad (2010) the traditional capitalist economic model tends to provide centralization and globalization of capital, creating inclusion and exclusion rules that leave segments of the population without access to products. Nowadays, it is argued more strongly the issues of sustainability and corporate social responsibility, which encourages the development, or rediscovery of alternative models of production and consumption.

Inclusive Capitalism is an economic vision that seeks to develop producers and consumers of the base of the social pyramid. Among the alternative answers is cooperativism. Social inclusion in the context of cooperative offers members opportunities to participate in the distribution of work, obtaining certain benefits such as the house itself and the country's income, within a system that benefits everyone and not just a layer of society.

This work proposes the analysis of the position of cooperatives from the perspective of the networked society, especially the assertion from Nohria and Eccles (1992) that all organizations are in networks, even if not using their connections. In principle, the social mission of housing cooperatives is at the organizer axis of a cooperation network, uniting organizations that produce the good (the property).

The cooperative production mode acts as rationalization vector of the production process, with advantages compared to individual work. It happens that the cooperation and commitment between the actors create synergies and more appropriate use of resources, while at the same time emerges incentive mechanisms and controls of opportunistic behavior. Such practices lead to the predominance of social ownership of the means of production and services, where the public outweighs the individual. The control of the enterprise and the power of decision belong to the society formed by members, rights-parity basis. The management of the task is attached to the cooperative that organizes the entire process, operates the economic strategies and deals with the surplus destination; in short, there is a unity between the ownership and the use of the means used to satisfy the immersed actors. Under these conditions the production methods are more efficient than traditional methods and costs are lower, allowing access to goods.

## 8.3 The interfaces between the cooperativism and the perspective of the network society

The concepts of cooperativism emerged from research of anthropologists and sociologists as Malinowski (1978) and Radcliffe Brown (1980) about different cultures. The thesis is that the essence of social relations would be given as a gift, understood as practices of giving, receiving, exchange and present, featuring reciprocity.

These ideas are close to those of Durkheim, always indicating collective relationships fostered by culture and moral established by individuals organized in a group, bringing a conducting wire, the alliance (Mauss, 2003), a concept close of ties (Burt, 1992).

Among the values that guide cooperative actions there is convergence in the literature on:

a) Use of wealth (resources) for the benefit of all;

b) Incentives to solidarity;

c) Respect to the merits and individual efforts;

d) Action guided by rationality;

e) Combat to selfishness.

These are items that in the concepts of networks appear as rational and economic (action guided by rationality and market power), or as social (incentive to solidarity). There is therefore a sustained line by authors on the review of rational, economic and social factors as fundamental in network configuration, with cooperative ethics.

At the interface between cooperativism and networks, there are the following convergences:

a) Reciprocity placed at the heart of action: people associate on a voluntary basis in order to meet economic, social and cultural needs;

b) The collective will of entrepreneurship: the individual return on investment is placed as a result of collective action;

c) The genesis and the actors involved: workers come together associatively from a social base of commitment, trust and cooperation; conducting collective production activities;

d) The organization of the group takes place within a dynamic engagement between the peers, with exchanges of knowledge, information and resources, favoring the creation of values and particular culture of each group and that social capital becomes important for the maintenance and project growth;

e) The inclusion and exclusion of cooperative members: it is by free will, with no need for formally breaking established contracts.

There is, as noted, integration between cooperative ethics and fundamentals of networks, especially when it is considered the following conceptual convergence of networks:

a) All companies are networked, whether they use or not its connections;

b) The actors are immersed in multiple relationships, which determine in part their behavior, goals and objectives;

c) There is a constant flow between network actors to exchange knowledge, experiences, information and resources;

d) The processes of social and economic flows of a particular group become part of their identity, contributing to the maintenance and growth of the group;

e) There is an integration of governance, interdependence, forms of communication, awareness of collective action and spontaneous input and output; with little need for formal contracts.

In the combination of the presence and content of variables, each group would present a formation feature, a network configuration. The guiding question of the work refers to the study of specific formation of the groups that participate in housing cooperatives in the state of São Paulo.

The starting point of the investigation is the statement that cooperatives are associations of people who are willing to work collectively with common goals and democratic decision-making processes, some as a way of managing public and social policies because it is based on collective action of various institutions of government and society; others, developing activities with specific forms of governance, with dynamic and complex structures and decentralized connections, in this case the cooperative relations and exchanges are predominant.

Although the hierarchy is most often missing in this model, the governance is a convergent factor, considering the model of Jones *et al.* (1997). For them, the network governance is how to coordinate joint activities, based on formal and informal contracts, to adapt to environmental contingencies and to coordinate and safeguard transactions through social and economic mechanisms (relationships). Without governance there is no relationship and decision process in networks, defining trends of the action of interconnected actors.

In the history of cooperative construction in Brazil, the government supported the process but then abandoned cooperatives, forcing the following by a self-managed way. It is argued in the article that because this shift in organizational environment, the cooperatives followed a distant way of cooperativism, creating classic relations of market (supply, demand, competition). So, along with the social objective of meeting people without income, there were production processes to other groups of buyers.

Literature review conducted by the authors showed that the social goal is not always present in the relationship of cooperatives with other organizations, which raises questions about the social role of companies and the distancing of the contemporary movement of a networked society, meaning cooperation.

"What is the dominant configuration arrangement between the organizations of the building cooperative?" is the guiding question

## 8.4 Methodology

The first task on the methodology consisted in raising and providing a summary of the characteristics of building cooperative processes in Brazil.

### 8.4.1 Housing cooperatives and building cooperative

Brazilian housing cooperatives are nowadays self-financing organizations, as the government withdrew its support. They are autonomous societies, controlled by their own members. They may enter into agreements with other institutions such as banks, construction companies and suppliers of materials and workmanship. In this movement to adapt to a reality without the government, social objectives were not always put in first place.

The problems of lack of integration, centralized management and inadequate operating results led the cooperatives to modify its mission and goals. In this reconfiguration, the housing cooperatives began to offer products to segments not in need of housing, creating relationships that are closer to the competition format in the market, than a cooperative system. In this particular field are involved the public sector, cooperatives, development entities such as the Organization of Cooperatives of Brazil-OCB and Sao Paulo-OCESP, National Service of Learning Cooperativism -SESCOOP, Unions of Housing Cooperatives-SINDICOOPERATIVAS, Regional Council of Engineering, Architecture and Agronomy-CREA and Regional Council of Real Estate Brokers CRECI, builders, developers, real estate, suppliers of materials and workmanship, banks and cooperative groups. It is a mixed group of organizations, some with strictly governmental functions, like development agencies and others with standard market performance. This set features the manifestations that characterize a network?

In social view of networks, the central element is the presence of trust relationships and commitment that create informal mechanisms of exchange and production (Belussi, Arcangeli, 1998).

As Singer (2005) explains, the old cooperatives in Brazil worked in this network format, but the survival conditions led to another format, with stronger competitive mechanisms than cooperative. The market forces are very strong and led cooperatives to adopt the traditional model to the detriment of other forms of production. The bureaucracy of the government and its strict laws turn unfeasible the social project, placing the cooperatives in a financial crash situation. Freedom of action in the market also means its removal of social ideals.

This market position has brought to cooperative production mode some advantages such as:

(A) Profit on capital management;

(B) No need to generate profit for owners, as the owners are cooperative members;

(C) Reduced costs for the consumer.

This self-management system has spread in the Brazilian states from the 1990s and the ultimate goal, not yet achieved, is that the products profits of higher classes fund projects of the most deprived classes. This has not occurred because the cooperative thinking is restricted to the group formed, which does not agree to have their capital for other ventures. Stated in another way, it is a cooperative system only for the individual well-being. There is a lack of the consciousness of sharing and reciprocity.

Thus, the relationship of cooperatives in the organization network seems to have acquired the competition stamp in the market, which means, with low cooperation, high formal governance and low fidelity. As an advantage, cooperatives have become free organizations in their management, which led to the phenomenon of some to develop much more than others.

These facts and analysis led to the next task, which was the field research.

**8.4.2 The planning and execution of the research.**

Housing cooperatives in the state of São Paulo were selected as the research field, investigating their relationship networks. In addition to primary sources, data was collected from secondary sources, such as documents, reports of meetings and news in newspapers.

For organizing and analyzing data a framework was developed, with some indicators of the presence of eight variables, selected for their importance in the academic literature on networks and cooperatives. Table 8.1 shows the dominant line with the concept, the core idea of what should be observed in the data and an example of the variable presence indicator. The complete table of the indicators is a work in progress here at the Universidade Paulista – UNIP.

**Table 8.1.Variables that characterize the network on the cooperative construction business**

| Variable | Content to be observed | Example of indicator |
|---|---|---|
| 1. Signs of the presence and content of commitment. | Attitudes and actions to achieve collective goals, or helping another actor, even if nothing is to win. | Regularly attend meetings and decisions. |
| 2. Signs of the presence and content of trust | Attitudes and actions in which the subject is exposed to the collective, or is dependent on the other, without resorting to formal control mechanisms. | Place itself in dependence on the other, showing their problems and asking for help. |

| 3. Signs of the presence and content of cooperation. | Attitudes and actions in which an individual engages and collaborates with each other without the need for formal control mechanisms | Cooperate or help others without formal contracts. |
|---|---|---|
| 4. Nature and forms of asymmetries solution | Differences of any nature those are relevant to the network structure and processes. | Solution modes of conflicts generated by differences in goals. |
| 5. Forms of governance | Set of explicit or implicit rules that place restrictions on behavior and protects the collective or individual resources. | Rules on admission and exclusion of actors in the smaller group. |
| 6. Presence and nature of interdependence | Collective events and processes that show the mutual dependence of enterprises by facilitating joint work to replace the individual work. | Signals of need of the resources that other actor has. |
| 7. Signal of the presence and dominance of strong and weak ties | They represent the possibility of greater or lesser immersion of the actors in the network, facilitating or not the relationships between the actors. | Frequency of Relationships. |
| 8. Economic strategies and performance | Types of tools to be used by the network to become more competitive in the market. | Diversity of products and services. |

**Source: Construction of the authors (2015).**

## 8.5. Submission of data

Data was collected from 146 documents available in organizations and databanks of libraries and the internet. Data was organized and analyzed according to Bardin's content analysis (1977), seeking the presence of the categories listed in Table 1.

The analysis indicates the convergence of the trend of cooperatives in actions with the members, seeking to recover an image of quality and transparency. There are several demonstrations in the reports, seminars and courses documents and news of local newspapers. It can be inferred that this movement is because the company image that only seeks profit is widespread among members.

This hypothesis was investigated in the questionnaires. Data was collected from 188 subjects who responded 35 statements on a Likert scale of five points, constructed from the indicators.

Table 8.2 shows the final result of the responses according to the scale. The analysis follows the criterion that the high percentage of agreement of a variable means a stronger presence in the configuration of group relations and its meaning of signal of the network format.

**Table 8.2. Responses to the questionnaire on the relations of the cooperative construction business organizations.**

| Variables | Strongly Disagree | Disagree | Neither agree nor disagree | Agree | Totally Agree |
|---|---|---|---|---|---|
| Commitment | 0% | 9% | 13% | 57% | 21% |
| Trust | 2% | 16% | 12% | 59% | 11% |
| Cooperation | 0% | 8% | 4% | 61% | 27% |
| Asymmetries | 0% | 11% | 13% | 60% | 17% |
| Governance | 2% | 5% | 14% | 60% | 19% |
| Interdependence | 0% | 9% | 10% | 52% | 29% |
| Strong and weak ties | 2% | 11% | 12% | 56% | 19% |
| Strategic and Economic Performance | 0% | 3% | 8% | 61% | 28% |

**Source: the authors (2015)**

The sum of the concordance of the responses (agree + totally agree) is always above 70%, and the Economic Strategy variable has the largest number (89%), followed by the Cooperation variable (88%). This data indicate that respondents perceive the cooperative building system in a network form, with economic goal.

Fifteen interviews were conducted with actors of organizations that operate more closely, such as banks, construction companies, government secretaries, cooperatives and cooperative members. The data was very precise and convergent to indicate an upcoming format of traditional market relationships, each seeking to realize their economic and strategic goals with almost complete absence of cooperative action consciousness.

The strongest category is the formal governance, originated in government and institution controls, each seeking to preserve their rights. This governance is far from that advocated by Jones *et al.* (1997) on governance which rises in the dynamics of networks.

## 8.6 Response to the research problem

The analysis showed convergence of networks and diversity.

With regard to convergence, all of them showed dominance of formal governance. They are networks with low interaction and integration among actors, with some isolated collective action efforts. The efforts are most evident in relations between the cooperative and its members.

Another convergence is the actors' efforts to meet their goals by following the business rules. This strong formal governance brings the actors closer, allowing some collective actions such as training and courses for members. However, each organization does its part without engaging in collective social projects.

The documents and interviews converged in indicating formal groupings, following market rules (competition), with few signals of format on networks. Already in questionnaires emerged stronger signs of networks. One reason is that most of the respondents of the questionnaires are cooperative members, who do not need to compete in the market.

Another convergent point with respect to the subgroup formed by the cooperative and the cooperative members is that it presents the strongest and most repetitive signals of social relations. Among all organizations' actors, the cooperative members are the ones that mobilize each other and links with other institutions to pursue their goals, which in the end is the collective goal of the network: deliver the property.

In relation to other actors in the business, the bank, the construction company, the cooperative, the government, the union, the accountability body and service providers; the data was inconsistent in showing a clear trend because in some networks the formal relations dominate; however in others, the presence of signals commitment to social activities was found.

Regarding to the differences between the networks, the governance may be one of the dividing lines where there is a progression that begins with more bureaucratic networks; networks focusing on business, even networks with more prominent social content. Next to this line of reasoning, there is the difference on the immersion of actors in the network. In more bureaucratic network, there are not organizations that make bridges, while in less bureaucratic networks there are organizations participating in various other networks.

Another point to be considered refers to the knowledge, awareness and attitude of collective action. Data appeared indicating the lack of vision and knowledge of actions in networks, although there is awareness of the need for a collective work, even in the bureaucratic networks that are more closed, without collective goals.

A strong government presence as a controller and the existence of financial and legal rules about business directly affect some of the organizations of the researched networks. As a result there are homogeneous processes, creating barriers to change, alliances and dissemination of cooperative principles. This inflexibility was most evident in the networks that work with government projects.

In response to the problem of research, about the presence of variables and the dominant format of the grouping of organizations, it is concluded that there is dominance of the principles of competition and that the networks and cooperatives variables are dispersed; from almost absence in basically bureaucratic networks, to a certain presence in networks of cooperatives that most moved away from government influence. The data support the statement of Nohria and Eccles (1992) that it is always possible to find networks format signals, even in a latent stage. In others words, the task of offering a house in a cooperative system presents the signals of networks, like interdependence, complexity, exchanges' needs, and governance; but the actors didn't develop the awareness about collective action.

The answer is interesting and shows that the configuration of the relationships of a group of organizations can change, even when there is strong interference and setting rules. Among the institutions there is the emergence of collective problems, such as the specific issue of an enterprise that mobilizes parties. The social, political and economic importance of the business involves that the organizations try to go beyond the pre-established rules, as the union of cooperative actors.

From the categories, it was noted that governance indicators and strategies were essentially factors present in cooperatives that use the self-management, indicating the solution of dependence and power of the state, going to a new process that is working in providing housing, offering goods for various social classes without settling only on government projects.

The construction and testing of these indicators is a methodological benefit of work because it was not found any similar in Brazilian academic literature.

## 8.7 Final comments

The objective was to analyze the configuration of networks from a set of selected variables of the theories on networks and on cooperativism. From the readings and previous reflections, we state that organizations working in cooperative construction business had lost the cooperative social objectives, adopting formats closer to isolated competition.

The data supported the assertion that it is possible to design networks of relationships, even when the collective cooperative action is almost absent. Secondly, this work brought a methodological benefit by presenting a framework of eight variables, operational definitions and indicators, which have proved to be able to differentiate configurations groups of organizations and, within each group, differentiate subgroups.

The work becomes important because in the bibliographical search was found that are rare the productions that propose the integration of variables. Secondly, but not least, the choice of the research field, the cooperative construction business, would trigger many studies for its social, economic and political importance, but it was found little work in the perspective of networks.

The data supported the statements from the perspective of the networked society (Nohria, Eccles, 1992; Castells, 1999), since it was always possible to find the signs of the presence of variables, although in varying degrees. The approach of the networked society is not widely used in the academic field, but it has the advantage of affirming the continued existence of social and economic flows of the actors in settings of all kinds, from designs that show well-organized networks, with rules and results, roles defined and settlement of conflicts; to networks that show the reverse situation, still in formation.

The choice of the cooperative construction field was due to its economic, social and political importance, especially in Brazil. Initial data collected by the authors showed that some cooperatives act as competitive companies offering various products on the market. This competitive position was confirmed in the data. Variables such as Economic Strategy and Governance showed strong presence, while social variables such as Trust and Cooperation rather appeared in the secondary data and interviews. Cooperatives that historically were more organized, with financial and material resources, with a good network of relationships, sought to survive away from the social cooperative ideal, organized in the form of self-management and act competitively in the market with product diversity and markets.

The results indicate that the conceptual model and research presented with their variables and indicators serve as basis for research in the areas of cooperativism, with the theoretical basis of networks. New research can improve the knowledge by incorporating and removing variables considering adding more relevant indicators.

As a methodological contribution, the instruments have been capable to discriminate different configurations. The different results obtained in the questionnaires can be explained by the majority interviewed cooperative members who do not need to use mental schemes of competition in the responses. Of course it remains the doubt whether the statements are valid or not, but the internal consistency of the direction of the responses does not put doubts about the instrument.

# References

BELUSSI, F., ARCANGELI, F. A typology of networks: flexible and evolutionary firms. Research Policy. v. 27, p. 415-428, 1998.

BURT, R. The Social Structure of Competition. In: NOHRIA, N.; ECCLES, R. (Eds.). Networks and Organizations: structure, form, and action. Boston: Harvard Business School Press, p. 491-520, 1992.

CASTELLS, M. The rise of network society. Cambridge: Willey Blackwell, v.1, 1999.

HART, S. O capitalismo na encruzilhada: as inúmeras oportunidades de negócios na solução dos problemas mais difíceis do mundo. Porto Alegre: Bookman, 2006.

JONES, C.; HESTERLY, W.., BORGATTI, S. A General Theory of Network Governance: Exchange Conditions and Social Mechanisms. Academy of Management Review, v. 22, n° 4, p. 911-945, 1997.

MALINOWSKI, B. Os argonautas do Pacífico ocidental. São Paulo: Ed. Abril Cultural, 1978.

MAUSS, M. Sociologia e Antropologia. São Paulo, Ed. Cosac & Naify, p. 401-422, 2003.

NOHRIA, N.; ECCLES, R. (Orgs). Networks and Organizations: structure, form and action, Boston: Harvard Business School Press: p. 1-22, 1992.

PRAHALAD, C. A riqueza na base da pirâmide: como erradicar a pobreza com o lucro. Porto Alegre: Bookman 2010.

RADCLIFFE-BROWN, A. O método comparativo em Antropologia Social In: ZALUAR, A. (org.). Desvendando máscaras sociais. Rio de Janeiro: Ed. Francisco Alves, p. 195-210, 1980.

SINGER, P. Introdução. In: MELLO, S. (Org.). Economia solidária e autogestão: encontros internacionais. São Paulo: Nesol, ITCP e PW, 2005._____Introdução à economia solidária. São Paulo: Editora Fundação Perseu Abramo, 2008.

# CHAPTER 9.

## THE CHALLENGES OF RESEARCH METHODOLOGY ON NETWORKS

**Ernesto M. Giglio,**
**Celso A. Rimoli,**
**Flávio R. Macau,**
**Renato Telles,**
**Marcio Cardoso Machado**

This chapter deals with some questions, challenges and possible responses of ways on how to conduct researches into networks.

Throughout the book, it was placed statements about what networks are, how they are characterized and how they manifest themselves. In the first chapter the categories that define the format networks were presented. The numerous applications of the research draft of these categories, held here in the Master's Program in Business Administration from Universidade Paulista- UNIP, have demonstrated their usefulness in indicating the configuration (or not) of network relations in a group of organizations.

In the various examples of research throughout the book, the reader must have realized questions about the validity of traditional forms of research, such as interviews and suggestions for alternative routes. Much of the international academic research on business networks have used collecting forms of interviews, questionnaires and data from secondary sources. These are traditional forms of research, when the question relates to the perceptions of the subjects, or explanations about processes, signs of presence or absence of factors chosen by the researcher. Are they sufficient for the network phenomenon considering its features?

In Chapter 1 it was stated that the networks are characterized by six categories: (A) Interdependence, (B) Complexity, (C) Exchanges' Need, (D) Awareness of the need for collective action, (E) the existence of collective goals, and (F) The presence of some rules, or joint action norms. In addition to these categories, the fact that the network is a group of people that relate with each other implies unpredictability and uncertainty of outcomes, that is, the past and the present are not guarantees of the future.

Let's look point to point. Some of these categories that indicate the network format, such as (C) Exchanges' Needs and (D) Awareness of the need for collective action can be investigated seeking the perception of the subjects. The (E) Existence of collective goals and (F) The presence of rules can also be investigated from questionnaires and interviews. The problems start in (A) Interdependence and (B) Complexity. It is not enough to ask a person if there is complexity, even because he or she would not know the concept.

Consider the following situation: You are researching about the interdependence and the complexity of a hospital system (not just a hospital, but the whole service is called hospital care, including laboratory testing companies, transportation, routine and extraordinary material supply, computer systems for scheduling and monitoring, equipment maintenance, to name a few). You know by data from secondary sources that the system is highly complex, which means, it works with joint action, sometimes synchronized, sometimes simultaneously. Its objective is to check the specificity of a selected network, which is considered a model of care compared to another network which is the subject of many complaints. It seems very clear that will not help to ask questions, or to apply questionnaires. You will need to track the various processes and try to infer where the advantages are of one problem and the other.

Well, then it's easy, because in production and logistics there are several tools for monitoring processes. True, except that none of them can include uncertainty, unpredictability and, most important in networks, forms of relationship between the parties. It is not enough just to follow the processes. It is necessary to monitor the relationship, the power games, the force of governance in controlling behaviors, the ever-shifting balance of relations of trust and commitment, freedom (or not) of people to act and innovate, the willingness to exchange information. In short, it is necessary to monitor the group dynamics, since the group may be well dispersed.

Now it's complicated. Even if the researcher has knowledge in research on group dynamics (which is very rare among administrators), he or she should resolve the question of how to follow the dynamics of a geographically dispersed group, with the existence of subgroups, performing different tasks, although affiliates.

In the Master's Program in Business Administration from Universidade Paulista-UNIP, in which all authors cited in this book work, or study, tests are being conducted on three lines as follow:

(A) By taking part in group meetings, whenever they occur. In Chapter 4, in the case of small farmers in northern Paraná, the group met every week, allowing to collect rich material that showed the social and religious rituals of the group, which would be virtually impossible in interviews (as it was not known of its existence, there was no reason to ask if everyone prayed before the meetings).

(B) Putting together a group when there are no regular meetings. The *focus group* technique, which is being tested in some opportunities by us[1] , reveals itself to be able to generate new data, not present in interviews and questionnaires.

(C) Following the contents of the collective communications. In certain business and cooperation networks we find a collective mode of communication (a collective email, for example), which allows to track content statement for all and it creates some inferences. One of our students brought to us a file containing messages from a collective email for a period of three years, which made it possible to see clearly a power game that was hardly reported in interviews.

(D) A path not yet tested by us, which exists in Psychology and Sociology, is tracking an actor in its routine, analyzing the moments of contact with the other actors in the network. The choice of actor to be followed is a critical problem of that instrument. One way to increase the certainty of choice is to analyze the relationship between the research objective and the place of the subject in the network (required prior information).

As can be seen, there are data collection paths seeking to directly observe the relationship and not the story. These paths are very rarely used, as verified

---

[1] There were two groups of environmental secretaries, discussing the implantation failure of rural environmental policies and three adult groups discussing the origins of piracy in Brazil. In the five groups emerged information that was not raised in interviews and questionnaires.

at the research. The research found which data collection and analysis techniques were being used in 156 studies on networks, in the congress called EnAnPAD, which is the largest congress of Administrators of Brazil.

In addition to these data, it was also placed information on the basis theory (which determines in part the methodology to be used) and the type of research that the author claimed to be using.

The summarized data can be seen in Table 9.1.

**Table 9.1. The analysis results of the research methodology of 156 articles of EnANPAD Congress, from four categories.**

| Basic theory | Q | Research Strategy | Q | Collection (c) and analysis (a) method | Q |
|---|---|---|---|---|---|
| Social Network and Social Capital | 35 | Descriptive | 83 | (c) Interviews | 95 |
| | | Qualitative | 71 | (c) Secondary data | 67 |
| Undefined | 34 | Case study | 69 | (c) Surveys | 49 |
| RBV and competencies | 23 | Exploratory | 40 | (c) Observation and follow up | 29 |
| | | Quantitative | 37 | | |
| Institutionalism | 19 | Explicative | 7 | (a) Content analysis | 22 |
| Economic theory | 19 | Transversal | 5 | (a) Descriptive statistic | 16 |
| Learning and cognition | 13 | Comparative analysis | 4 | | |
| Resources dependency | 13 | Transversal analysis | 4 | | |

**Source: Giglio, Hernandes, 2012, p.89.**

In the item of Research Strategy there is a dominance of descriptive, qualitative and case studies researches. In terms of scientific development, these strategies are most appropriate when science is at an early stage of investigation of a phenomenon, which does not seem to be on the networks subject case, which has scientific literature for at least three decades. A detailed analysis of the discussions and conclusions showed that only 3 works (out of 156) performed interpretations and tried to create models, as a forward step in scientific knowledge.

On data collection techniques the great convergence is the interview, followed by secondary data (basically gathering bibliographic data and documents of the companies) and questionnaires. Do those forms of data collection have the ability to capture the phenomenon of relationships in networks? On this issue Marsden (1990) coined the term *cognitive network* to indicate that the interviews data show the vision that the subject has about the network, which is different from the factual dynamic of the network. Accepting this statement, it appears that a significant number of research generated knowledge about the cognitive processes of apprehension of the network phenomenon and not on networks as explained.

The data collection by observation and monitoring appeared 29 times, but could not possibly get information about how it was carried out the monitoring and what, exactly, was being watched. Authors such as Latour (2005) and Tichy, Tushman, Fombrun (1979) argue that monitoring is a valid technique to collect the relationships in the network as long as the unit of study is the flow.

On data analysis techniques, it showed two dominant forms: a content analysis and descriptive statistics. Here is found consistency with the dominant research strategies (descriptive and qualitative). As Bardin (1977) often cited when this technique is used, the analysis should evolve until building the statements, hypotheses, models, that enable the next step in the investigation. As already mentioned, this occurred in only 3 cases.

The conclusion is that the 156 works on networks, presented during a decade in this annual congress, did not add scientific knowledge, did not innovate in research methodology, and, what can be worrisome, created conclusions on the structure, dynamics, problems and solutions of networks that can easily be questioned. Once most of the papers presented at this conference are graduate students, repeating the ideas of their advisors, it is a concern (and the challenge) of scientific knowledge construction in the Networks area.

In the pages of this book we modestly point out some ways. First (Chapter 1) we indicate the categories witch define the format, or the state of networks. In our literature searches to date we have found no work that has made this conjunction. In chapters 2, 3 and 4 we present some categories (power, governance, trust, commitment) that may constitute the pillars of the dynamics of networks. In other words, we affirm that it is difficult to understand the processes of a group and the behavior of people in this group if those categories are not considered.

Chapter 5 has developed some concepts and research on the interface between business networking, marketing, innovation and results. For the authors of this book, have become increasingly clear that the boundaries between the various manifestations of networks are unclear and probably do not exist, being only a research limited effort. Business networks, cooperation networks, social networks, policy networks may be intertwined, as a polygon showing one facet at a time. Furthermore, there is an interdisciplinary between networks and marketing which is little discussed.

In Chapters 6 and 7 we show two key topics emerging from the network phenomenon, learning and brand diffusion on networks, placing them within the matrix originated in previous chapters, on the characteristics of the networks and their relationship bases. Finally, this last chapter, we alert to the need to innovate in ways of research.

Chapter 8 showed how environmental conditions and government interference can lead organizations that have social and cooperative objectives to give up these objectives in support of a survival in the market. The investigated housing cooperatives operating today, in an isolated competition format, offering products for the middle and upper class in Brazil, far removed from the proposed social housing actions.

Thus we believe we are offering an initial matrix of thought and research design for the advancement of knowledge about networks. The proposal, in the form of a design, can be seen in Figure 9.1, where one finds the conditions that indicate the network format (six categories), the subsystem of relations between the actors (with the four categories we consider the bases or axes of networks) and two outputs of the system (among other possible) resulting from the combination of the above factors.

**Figure 9.1. The matrix of thought and research on networks in its various manifestations (business, cooperation, social, etc.).**

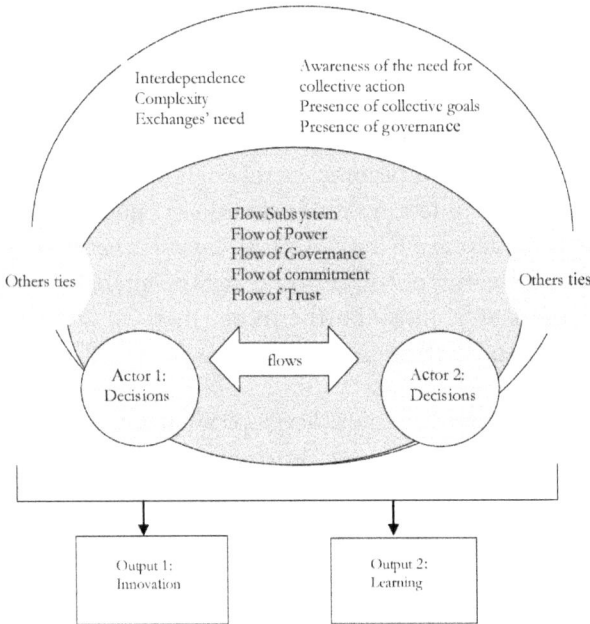

Interdependence
Complexity
Exchanges' need

Awareness of the need for
collective action
Presence of collective goals
Presence of governance

Flow Subsystem
Flow of Power
Flow of Governance
Flow of commitment
Flow of Trust

Others ties

Others ties

Actor 1:
Decisions

flows

Actor 2:
Decisions

Output 1:
Innovation

Output 2:
Learning

**Source: Construction of authors, 2015.**

On modes of investigation, we are convinced that the principles of complexity, such as uncertainty and unpredictability, are competent to provide a way of building research plans on networks that accept the momentary, the order and disorder at the same time and the primacy systemic relations, instead of strict causal relationships.

Structuring the network phenomenon as a system has some advantages over traditional designs of cause and effect, such as the ability to investigate interrelationships, which is interesting and appropriate in dynamic networks.

With a follow-up technique can be seen, for example, a weekly meeting of a group, the evolution of the positions, the contents circulating, exchanges of information, the formation of subgroups of interest, among other possibilities.

It is not, of course, to impose a path, but to indicate some possibilities unexplored so far in the literature on what a network is, what are its characteristics and how to research on it. We hope to have contributed in this way.

# References

BARDIN, L. Análise de conteúdo. Lisboa: Edições 70, 1977.

GIGLIO, E.; HERNANDEZ, J. Discussões sobre a metodologia de pesquisa sobre redes de negócios presentes numa amostra da produção científica brasileira e proposta de de um modelo orientador. Revista Brasileira de Gestão e Negócios – RGBN, v.14, n.42, p. 78-101, 2012.

LATOUR, B. Reassembling the social. Oxford: Oxford Press, 2005.

MARSDEN, P. Network data and measurement. Annual Review of Sociology, Palo Alto, v. 16, p. 435-463, 1990.

TICHY, N.; TUSHMAN, M.; FOMBRUN, C. Social networks analysis for organizations. Academy of Management Review, Biarcliff Manor, v. 4, n. 4, p.507-519, 1979.

# Presentation of the main authors, in alphabetical order.

### Celso A. Rimoli

PhD of Business Administration from the Faculty of Administration and Economics, University of São Paulo. Professor and Graduate Program Researcher in Business Administration from Universidade Paulista - UNIP, which develops courses and research on networks. Participated for two years in research at SPRU, University of Sussex, UK. Nowadays, he seeks to build a model of integration between the Networks, Marketing and Innovation fields.

### Ernesto M. Giglio

PhD in Business Administration from the Faculty of Administration and Economics, University of São Paulo and Post Doctorate in Business Administration from the Federal University of Lavras. Professor and Graduate Program Researcher in Business Administration from Universidade Paulista - UNIP, which develops courses and research on networks. Nowadays, he seeks to build a conceptual model of the network organization of states, which must be more than a structural analysis.Current research fields are tourism networks, solidarity markets and small farmer networks.

### Flavio R. Macau

PhD in Operations Strategy by Getulio Vargas foundation.Professor, Researcher and Coordinator of the Graduate Program in Business Administration from Universidade Paulista - UNIP, which develops courses and research on networks. Nowadays, he seeks to build conceptual models regarding knowledge management in networks and strategies in networks. His current research field is agribusiness, particularly in export networks.

## Marcio C. Machado

Postdoctoral fellowship from the Technological Institute of Aeronautics.PhD in Industrial Engineering from the University of Sao Paulo. He was Professor and Researcher at the Instituto Tecnológico de Aeronáutica - ITA. He is currently a professor at the Catholic University of Sao Paulo and Professor and Researcher at the Graduate Program of Universidade Paulista - UNIP. He has experience in Production Engineering with emphasis in Aeronautical Maintenance on the following topics: lean, product development, quality, logistics, PCP and maintenance management. Nowadays, he seeks to build interfaces between the concepts of networks and the concepts of Supply Chain.

## Renato Telles

PhD in Business Administration from  the Faculty of Administration and Economics, University of São Paulo.Business Consultant. Researcher and Professor of the Graduate Program in Business Administration from Universidade Paulista - UNIP, which develops courses and research on networks and clusters.Currently he is developing research on clusters based on the concepts of complex adaptive systems, seeking to build conceptual and methodological models. Research fields involve food and textile industries.

# Presentation of the contributing authors

The contributing authors are students and alumni of the Graduate Program in Business Administration from the University Paulista-UNIP, who contributed with their research.

Augusto C. D'Arruda

Carlos Eduardo Santos

Cláudia Rosa M. Velozo

Cristiane Veloso

Eduardo Clemente Alves

Eliana C. Tarricone

Filipe M. G. Freitas

José Roberto Gamba

Léo Eduardo P. Noronha

Maria Carolina de Arruda

Nilson Bertoli

Saturnina A. Silva Martins

Thaís C. Ravasi

Walter Cardoso Sátyro

www.ingramcontent.com/pod-product-compliance
Lightning Source LLC
Chambersburg PA
CBHW050506210326
41521CB00011B/2353